C000179030

Walk!

Lanzarote

by

David & Ros Brawn

DISCOVERY WALKING GUIDES LTD

Walk! Lanzarote
First Edition - June 2004

Copyright © 2004

Published by
Discovery Walking Guides Ltd
10 Tennyson Close, Northampton NN5 7HJ,
England

Maps
Maps are adapted from Lanzarote Tour & Trail
Super-Durable Map (ISBN 1-899554-95-5)
published by **Discovery Walking Guides Ltd**

Photographs
*All photographs in this book were taken by the
authors, Ros & David Brawn, with the exception of
that on P.116, which was taken by Alan Lambert.

Front Cover Photographs

Playa de Famara
Walks 31 & 32

Hidden Barrancos
Walk 14

Haria Valley
Walk 24

Femés Ridge
Walk 15

ISBN 1-899554-94-7

Text and photographs* © David & Ros Brawn

Walk! Lanzarote

CONTENTS

BACKGROUND

INTRODUCTION

THE WALKS

ACKNOWLEDGEMENTS

In 1995 we published our first guide for walkers to Lanzarote. 'Lanzarote, A Discovery Walking Guide' proved popular and sold well, allaying our initial doubts that Lanzarote would be an attractive walking destination. Since then we have received a steady trickle of letters from users of that first guide, who let us how much they had enjoyed the guide, and sometimes including suggestions for more routes. Our sincere thanks go to these walkers, as without their feedback this publication might not have happened.

With an ever busier research, writing and mapping schedule, we looked for a local walker and author to research this book for us. We were pleased to find Alan Lambert who took to our GPS mapping system like a duck to water and rapidly completed a collection of routes. All was going according to plan, but then we suddenly lost contact. Emails and phone calls went unanswered, and we still have no idea where he is. Fortunately, he had sent us some of his data and ideas for routes. So, we rearranged our schedule and walked the island ourselves in early 2004 over two research periods, and found it enjoyable, informative and at times, exhausting. We would like to thank Alan for his part in this book, and hope that he (or someone who knows him) sees this book and encourages him to get in touch.

THE AUTHORS

David & Ros Brawn

David and Ros have lived and worked in England, Papua New Guinea and the Seychelles before settling for a number of years in Tenerife. David's first published books were accountancy texts.

David and Ros have been walking and writing for Discovery Walking Guides since it began, researching guides for most of the seven Canary Islands, the Balearic Islands, Malta, Gozo, Madeira, the Alpujarras and Aracena. More recently they have surveyed and mapped a number of these regions using satellite navigation equipment combined with cartographic software.

Considering themselves as semi-permanent travellers, they divide their non-research time between Spain and Northampton, England.

David is a member of the British Cartographic Society.

David & Ros are the authors of a number of publications to various destinations including:
Tour & Trail Maps
Tour & Trail Super-Durable Maps
Walkers' Maps
34/35 Walks Guidebooks
Walk! Guidebooks
David is also the author of:
GPS The Easy Way

BACKGROUND

HISTORY

Lanzarote and Fuerteventura's first inhabitants were the *Majos* (or Mahos), the approximate equivalent of the *Guanches* in the western Canary Islands. It is thought that they led a relatively uneventful existence until 1402, when the Norman *conquistador* Jean de Bethencourt arrived, befriending the *Majo* leader and taking peaceful control of the island from a camp in **Rubicón**, soon passing power to his nephew Maciot, the founder of the island's original capital **Teguise**.

The *Majos* named the island 'Titerroygatra', which translates as 'coloured hills', a name which would be just as appropriate today, though its current name is an adaptation of the name of an influential immigrant, Lancelotto Malocello.

GEOGRAPHY

Lanzarote is the most northerly and least mountainous of the Canary Islands, its highest point being 675 metres, **Peñas del Chache**, unfortunately taken over by the military and off limits to walkers. Its 169 kilometres of coastline varies between yellow and black beaches, cliffs and lava *malpaís*, offering some photogenic scenes. The island has been repeatedly shaped by volcanic activity, the most famous being the 1730-36 eruptions which formed **Timanfaya**, and the last in 1824 which created the volcanoes of **Tinguatón**, **Tao** and **Nuevo del Fuego**.

CLIMATE & AGRICULTURE

Lanzarote's close proximity to Africa is apparent in its weather. The dry, desert-like climate is interrupted by a few rainy days, typically in winter and early spring, but not amounting to much; for this reason the island's water supply comes from desalination plants. The modest height of Lanzarote's hills is insufficient to benefit from the humidity of the trade winds, but even so the lack of rain has not deterred the islanders from devising methods of growing a wide range of fruits and vegetables.

Particularly remarkable are the *zocos*, notably in **La Geria** where the black volcanic *picón* (ash) filters moisture to the roots and mulches the soil beneath, while keeping the plants cool. This is a windy island, and the agricultural plots are often protected from the prevailing winds by horseshoe shaped walls. When easterly winds blow they bring hot, dust-laden *calimas*, best avoided by staying indoors.

thi´ngy (noun)

1. Inanimate object that the speaker has temporarily forgotten the name of.
2. Large, or over large, man-made object of no discernible use prominently displayed in a public place, notably in the centre of large roundabouts. Associated with the Canary Island of Lanzarote and its most famous citizen César Manrique (artist, 1919-1992).

César Manrique's legacy to Lanzarote is seen in many aspects of the island's life, visibly in the squat white painted houses with green or blue window shutters but most notably in the 'sculptures' adorning roundabouts on the island's main roads. Whether you consider these constructions as art seems open to question. Is the huge green tin-can cactus, outside the gardens in **Guatiza**, art? Or is it simply an advertisement in the same genre that American and Australian businesses use, equivalent to a giant 'hamburger' outside a burger bar?

Some residents are very defensive over these Thingys, believing that anything

César Manrique promoted must be good for the island. You will have plenty of opportunities to form your own Thingy opinion as you travel round. Our rating of which Thingy is worthy of its name is:

Recommended:-

- 'Madonna' wind measurement Thingy on the **Arrieta** roundabout. The workings of this Thingy are missed by car drivers so park nearby and walk back to the roundabout to see it in action.

- 'Monument to the Campesino' on the first LZ1 roundabout north of the **Arrecife** *circunvalacion.* Build it on a big scale, and even

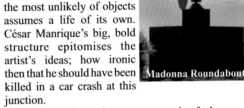

the most unlikely of objects assumes a life of its own. César Manrique's big, bold structure epitomises the artist's ideas; how ironic then that he should have been killed in a car crash at this junction.

Madonna Roundabout

- 'Rock Finger' at the western end of the new **Matagorda-Playa Honda** promenade; see Walk 1. An elegant post-Manrique Thingy, if a bit on the small size compared to the dictionary definition.

- 'Radar' Thingy on the airport road system. A post César Manrique installation usually missed by drivers attempting to negotiate the lane-switching required to escape from the airport.

Airport Radar Thingy

"Art, or junk?" the jury is out:-

- 'Twin pillars' on the end of the **Costa Teguise** dock; Walk 3. Certainly tall enough to count as thingys but is their weathered intergalactic nature in the César Manrique mould?
- 'Defunct R2D2' beside the Twin Pillars; Walk 3. Rendered insignificant by the towers?
- 'Toast Rack/Wind Chime' on the **Tahiche** LZ1 roundabout. Shouldn't a Thingy be rather more solid and less ethereal?
- 'Sailing Dingy' on roundabout at **Puerto Calero**; Walk 2. Modern concrete sculpture but perhaps too lifelike, and not abstract enough to rank as a Thingy.

Puerto Calero's Sailing Dinghy

- 'Giant Hill Sculpture' in the **Barranco de la Higuera**; Walks 17 & 22. Certainly big enough, and sufficiently devoid of discernible use to count as a Thingy, but only a small number of adventurous walkers will get to see it.

In the bin, or Paul Merton's Room 101:-

Giant (fake) cactus marks the Jardín de Cactus

- 'Giant Sun Lounger' east of **Costa Teguise** dock; Walk 3. Rusting steel and crumbling concrete do not a true Thingy make.
- 'Tin-Can Cactus' outside the **Guatiza** Cactus Garden. Surely this Lanzarote equivalent of the giant glass-fibre Lobster placed on top of a sea food restaurant, or giant cockroach on a pest exterminator's van, cannot be considered art as it is an advertising symbol. The idea of a Thingy is that it has no discernible use.
- 'Iron Horse' on the western sea front of **Arrecife**; Walk1. An example of the modernist Spanish Thingy style possibly encouraged by César Manrique's original Thingys.

Lobster Traffic Island

- 'Ship's Ventilator rubbish bins on the sea front park; Walk1. Not really Thingys but why waste a chance to have a go at a good idea which becomes an eyesore due to a lack of maintenance?
- 'Lobster' traffic island between **Punta Mujeres** and **Jameos del Agua**. As with the Cactus, an advertisement.

Thingys are now firmly embedded in Lanzarote culture and may proliferate as more large roundabouts are being built. Private examples can be seen as you travel around the island and while these clearly have no discernible use, they are neither large enough, nor prominently displayed in a public place, to count as Thingys.

There are many 'artistic' style houses around the island adorned/decorated with many 'no discernible use' items. Currently we do not classify these as Thingys, not even when they have an old Huey helicopter fuselage as part of the 'construction' (**Casitas de Femés**).

FIRST IMPRESSIONS

If you are used to Mediterranean island destinations, or you've visited the western Canary Islands, your first arrival on the island might come as a bit of a shock. As your plane approaches the airport, you'll have an impression of barren starkness, relieved only by clusters and scatterings of cloned, squat white buildings, clustered thickly here and there on the coastline.

But, give yourself a few hours to adapt, and you should begin to appreciate the subtleties of what is a chunk of African desert, overlain with volcanic spewings. The lava fields themselves have a certain weird beauty, and once you get over the withdrawal symptoms caused by the lack of trees, you'll find that Lanzarote is an island offering more colour and contrast than you might have assumed. The volcanic cones come in a variety of hues, and many parts of the coastline are dramatic and photogenic.

Although Lanzarote might not appear at first glance to offer much variety or challenge for walkers, this book will change your opinion.

WHEN TO GO

If you want to walk, avoid the summer months of July, August and September. It's hot, dusty and suitable for beach and water sports only. Be aware that, although Lanzarote has very little precipitation, you can hit some wet days; while completing research from February to April, there were four or five wet days. There were also a couple of *calimas*, the unpleasant hot, dust-laden east wind which picks up half the African deserts and then dumps it on the island. The skies darken with the suspended dust, and if you are a contact lens wearer or an asthma sufferer, you'll feel miserable. We wouldn't recommend walking in a *calima*, which can last anything from a couple of days to a week.

WHERE TO STAY

Almost all the accommodation is in the tourist resorts of **Costa Teguise**, **Puerto del Carmen** and **Playa Blanca**. The first two of these have the advantage of being close to the airport, having a reasonable bus service, and plenty of the usual tourist things, such as beaches, bars and shops. **Playa Blanca** is the place for you if you want to be near the ferry port for Fuerteventura, but it's a long way from everywhere else, and has a limited bus service. Sporting types can stay on the north coast at **Club La Santa** although there is not much distraction apart from within the complex itself.

GETTING AROUND THE ISLAND

There's a bus timetable in the back of this book, but be aware that these can change, so check when you arrive, either at the Biosphere Information Office which faces you as you emerge from the baggage hall at the airport, or in the **Puerto del Carmen** tourist office. Some bus routes operate only on work days, or only on Sundays (market specials), and some towns and villages have only three or four buses a day. If you intend to use buses to access and return from walks, check the times first, and be prepared to use taxis.

Easiest is to hire a car, easily available and at reasonable rates. When using a car for linear walking routes, try to link up with like-minded walkers with another hire car and use the 2CSK method - see page 16 for an explanation.

If you need a taxi when you are not near a tourist resort, ask in a bar and they will usually phone for you - but do buy a drink as well.

CÉSAR MANRIQUE

Within hours of the visitor's first arrival on Lanzarote, the influence of César Manrique will already be obvious. The plain white, low-level buildings in traditional, unadorned style with their dark green doors and windows, and the sometimes startling sculptures that form traffic roundabouts, all bear witness to the singular effect this individual had - and still has - on the development of the island.

Born in **Arrecife** in 1919, he was a volunteer with Franco's troops during the Spanish Civil War of 1936-39 before he became an artist, holding his first exhibition in his home town at the age of 21. Moving to the mainland, he studied at the Academia de Belles Artes de San Fernando in Madrid where he developed his abstract art ideas. Enthusiastic reactions to his first serious exhibition of 1954 led to its tour of galleries in many European cities, followed by a tour of the USA following the invitation of Nelson Rockefeller.

In 1968, he was ready to return home, armed with ideas for the conservation of Lanzarote, and for the development of the island in a controlled manner. He was responsible for the banning of roadside advertising hoardings in the countryside, and urged the powers that be to lay down strict building rules to encourage traditional low level development.

Under his guidance, the **Jameos del Agua** caves were turned into a tourist attraction and an underground theatre, and he was also the force behind the **Jardín de Cactus**, which although it contains the real thing, is oddly marked by an outrageously fake, giant cactus in its car park. He had more than a hand in many other projects on the island, including the **Mirador del Río**, and the **Restaurante del Diablo** inside the **Montañas del Fuego** where the volcanic energy is used to cook the food.

Manrique - Monumento al Campesino

His main residence during these years was **Taro de Tahiche**, north of **Arrecife**, now the **Fundación de César Manrique**, since his surreal death in a road traffic accident in 1992 on the very roundabout that he had alerted the authorities to as dangerous. His vision continues under the auspices of the El Guincho environmental group.

In 1993, UNESCO recognised his efforts in preserving the natural environment of the island by declaring the entire island a World Biosphere Reserve.

PARQUE NACIONAL DE TIMANFAYA

An incredible eruption of cataclysmic proportions and lasting six years began on 1 September 1730. Centred in the south of the island, the **Montañas del Fuego** or Mountains of Fire, caused devastation to an area of 200 sq. km. The ground is still hot to the touch in places, and a party trick by the guides is to toss a dry bush into a crevasse whereupon it is instantly consumed by fire. The feeling is that the boiling molten magma is still close enough for discomfort. The **Restaurante del Diablo** built on the **Islote de Hilario** area within the park, uses the power of the volcano to barbecue the food, though it tastes no different to other forms of cooking and you do pay extra for this novelty.

Access to the park is restricted to cars and tour coaches (entrance fee payable), although there are guided walks available. If you would like to join one of these, apply at the **Centro de Visitantes** (Visitors' Centre) on the LZ 67 road, south of **Mancha Blanca**, in person or by phone on 928 840839. They offer a two hour, three kilometre 'Caldera de Tremesana' walk, usually on Mondays, Wednesdays and Fridays, (See Walk 18, 'Tremesana Guided Walk') and a tougher 'Ruta del Litoral' lasting about five hours and covering a distance of 9 kilometres which is arranged according to demand.

You can also take a coach tour from the parking area, taking in the weird volcanic landscapes, though you might find the multi-lingual commentary and taped music which accompany the tour irritating, and it is frustrating not to be have the freedom to walk independently in these unique surroundings.

LANZAROTE'S SALT

Salinas del Janubio

Lanzarote produces about one third of the salt it needs, but the industry is not as important as it once was. The **Salinas del Río**, (see Walk 30, 'Salinas del Río') almost on the island's most north-westerly point, are thought to have been constructed in the fifteenth century and are shown on maps drawn in 1590. The quantities of salt produced from this area were more than sufficient to serve the island's needs and the excess was sold to La Palma and Tenerife. Until 1775, these salt pan were the only ones on Lanzarote, but from that time on several were constructed to cash in on the growing market. The **Salinas del Agujero** were constructed in 1940, near **Los Cocoteros** which , together with the **Salinas del Janubio** are the principal remaining commercial salt pans on the island.

The most scenic of the *salinas* are the **Salinas del Janubio** which exists thanks to the volcanic eruptions of 1730, when molten lava formed the walls of the natural lake of **Laguna de Janubio**. Although salt production has declined in the last few decades, the *salinas* have become important as havens for bird life.

CACTI & COCHINEAL

Naturalised in all the Canary Islands, the Prickly Pear cactus (opuntia) was introduced as a useful hedging plant whose edible fruits are edible are collected by those prepared to risk being impaled on its sturdy spikes; you may see Canarians collecting these bright red or orange fruits with the aid of wooden tongs. Prickly Pears also proved to be the most popular host plant for the cochineal beetle, which led to a thriving cottage industry in the valuable dark red dye harvested from these insects which are dried and ground. The development of artificial colourings almost killed the industry, but in recent years some manufacturers - especially of drinks, foodstuffs and cosmetics - have returned to this natural dye.

Cactus farm near Guatiza

The cochineal beetles give away their presence by the protective white powder that they exude around themselves as they feed off the cactus sap. There are few naturalised cacti in the Canaries without a few of these telltale signs of infestation, and in a few villages including **Guatiza** and **Mala** they are still farmed despite the extremely labour-intensive nature of the industry, each tiny bug being collected by hand.

GOATS

Goats are survivors, and can live quite happily on a diet of tough, wizened and spiny plants at which any sheep would turn up its nose. The ideal livestock for an arid and unforgiving landscape, they have been part of the way of life for many generations, and although the estimated numbers have varied between the 14,000 of the 1970s and a low of around 3000 or fewer in the 1990s, their numbers are now on the increase, with an estimated 15,000 or so surviving perfectly happily on what might appear to be barren desert. It would be easy to make the assumption that these are wild creatures, but most have owners, as the presence of goatherds proves.

Traditionally a source of meat, milk, cheese, wool, skins, tallow for candles and a host of herbal cures and remedies, the goat was historically an essential factor in the survival of Lanzarote's early settlers. These days there is a healthy market for goat's cheese and meat, and a limited demand for crafts using goat's wool and skins, mainly for souvenir items. You would be unlucky not to see a herd of these multi-patterned creatures while walking on the island, and you'll probably envy them their sure-footedness and easy tackling of slippery slopes.

If you want a change from walking (or the beach) there are several attractions to visit. The island's best natural wonders have been turned into profit making ventures, including the **Montañas del Fuego** (09.00 to 17.45) inside the **Parque Nacional de Timanfaya**, the **Jardín de Cactus** (10.00 to 17.45), the **Mirador del Río** (10.00 to 17.45), the **Jameos del Agua**, (09.30 to 18.45), a huge volcanic tube inside which is a lake, restaurant, bars and a theatre, and the **Cueva de los Verdes** (10.00 to 18.00), another part of the same massive volcanic tube which has been kept in a more natural state.

There are several museums of anything from traditional and contemporary art, wine, agriculture, Lanzarote emigrants and local crafts.

There's a wide choice of boat trips from sightseeing to diving or fishing, and you can hop over to Fuerteventura from **Playa Blanca** in 25-40 minutes depending on the ferry, or see the tiny island of La Graciosa, reached by ferry from **Orzola** in about 25 minutes. Camel treks and horse riding are available, and the relatively flat terrain and quiet roads are ideal for cycling, with bicycle hire offered by several companies. Costa Teguise has a golf course. (See 'Useful Information' in the back of this book for more on activities)

Los Hervideros

Free attractions include the **Salinas del Janubio** (see notes on the island's salt industry earlier in this introduction), the coastline at **Los Hervideros** (the boiling springs), north of the salt pans where the sea boils and spouts through lava fissures. The jagged lava has been tamed into a series of narrow paths which lead among the lava and caves, and if the sea is rough expect to get a shower as the sea is forced up through natural blowholes.

Charco de los Clicos

Also worth a visit is the bay (really, half a volcanic crater) known as **Charco de los Clicos** near the settlement of **El Golfo**. And of course, all the sights experienced when following the walks in this book should be added to your list.

Trees are scarce on Lanzarote, and where they do grow, it is thanks to careful planting and sustained watering. Some of the best plantings are in hotel gardens, where they provide a valuable mini-habitat for bird and insect life.

Because the volcanic history of the island is still relatively recent, swathes of its surface are still littered with lava in one of its forms. These areas of *malpaís* show signs of the process of breaking down into smaller particles that will eventually become soil, as the colourful colonies of lichen prove.

La Geria grape fields

In other areas where volcanic ash rather than rock and lava streams covered them, (such as **La Geria**, Walk 22), fertile soil lies beneath black duvets of fine ash, which serve to protect the roots of Malvasia grape vines, figs and other crops while drawing moisture from the cooler night air, which then percolates downwards. This method of mulching with a thick layer of ash has been adopted for agriculture of all kinds often used with the horseshoe-shaped low walls or *zocos* which give additional protection from the prevailing winds.

The Haría Valley

The dampest part of Lanzarote, the north, has the deepest and most workable soil. The little town of **Haría** (Walk 24, 'The Forgotten Trail' and Walk 25, 'Circuit of Haría'), sits in a fertile bowl where many types of fruit and vegetable crops are grown. The whole valley is dotted with Phoenix canariensis palms, and the roadsides are sparsely lined by white or pale pink Tamarix africana.

Look in the north of the island, especially around the **El Risco de Famara** and **Haría** areas, for the island's own endemic miniature version of sea-lavender, Limonium puberulum. Easier to spot is the white tajinaste, Echium decaisnei which can reach 1½ metres in height, and the bright yellow Sonchus pinnatifidus which resembles a giant dandelion. Another yellow giant is the fennel, Ferula lancerottensis, also an endemic.

Mesembryanthemum crystallinum is a big name for the small, ground-hugging ice-plant which is common in many parts of the island, once used in the production of a type of soda.

The bibliography at the back of this book suggests further reading on Lanzarote's plant life.

We have worked hard to ensure that our routes are as accessible as possible, but a combination of Lanzarote's sparse rural bus service and the landscape mean that we have a number of long linear routes. Walks 12, 16, 18 (unofficial version), 20, 26, 27, and 31 are just such routes. For the very energetic you might consider walking there and back again, or on routes 16, 26 and 27 you could invest in a taxi for the return. You could swap Walk 12's slog up from **Yaiza** or **Uga** for our new Walk 13 circular route based on **Femés**.

2CSK is our recommended solution to the problem of accessibility on linear routes. Basically you need two walking couples/groups, each with its own hire car (**2C**).
The couples/groups get together and agree which linear routes they will walk, and when.
On the day of the walk each group drives to one end of the linear route, locks the car, and starts walking the route.
When the two groups meet, you swap/exchange car keys (**SK**), and at the end of the walk drive the waiting hire car back to your base.

2CSK is the method normally used for the **Tremesana**/**Timanfaya** official guided walk, when the guides drive to the ends of the walk, swap keys when they meet, and at the end you return in the other minibus. In practice, never underestimate the ability of the other group to become confused as to what they should be doing. You will only know if things have gone 'belly up' when you arrive at the end of that long route, not having crossed with anybody, to find no car!
Among the things that can go wrong are:-

• The other group get lost and never find the other end of the route.
• The other group believe that you are walking a different linear route and start out on the wrong route.
• One, or both groups get lost during the route and miss each other.
• After swapping keys one, or both groups forget the car description, and/or parking place; spending hours searching for a car that fits the key.

These are the main causes of 2CSK failure but we are sure there are plenty of others. But when it works, it's a great way of seeing otherwise inaccessible regions of the island. The key to success is planning. Write everything down. Make sure both groups have a good map (**Lanzarote Tour & Trail Super-Durable Map**) and guide book. If you have mobiles, make sure you have their number. Write down the details of the other hire car and ask where it has been parked when you meet.

If you get the choice of which end to start the 2CSK routes, then our advice is:-

Walk 12. Start at **Femés**; a stiff unrelenting ascent but wonderful descent down to **Yaiza**/**Uga**. Essential that you know where the other car is parked in the town.

Walk 16. Start at **Femés**, and after a stiff ascent it's all downhill. Be aware that it is very easy to miss each other amongst the wonderful bays and wastelands at the south of the **Rubicón** desert. Essential to know where the other car is parked in **Playa Blanca**.

🔑 Walk 18. Either start point is equally agreeable.

🔑 Walk 20. Start from **Playa de la Madera**, then you are close to refreshments in **El Golfo** or **Yaiza** when you finish.

🔑 Walks 26 and 27. Our preference is to walk towards **Teguise**, park on main road for easy location.

🔑 Walk 31. Start from **Yé**, unless you enjoy a long uphill slog with an even steeper finish.

SYMBOLS RATING GUIDE

 our rating for effort/exertion:-
1 very easy   **2** easy   **3** average
4 energetic   **5** strenuous

 approximate **time** to complete a walk (compare your times against ours early in a walk) - does not include stopping time

 approximate walking **distance** in kilometres

 approximate **ascents/descents** in metres
(N = negligible)

 circular route

 linear route

 risk of **vertigo**

 refreshments (may be at start or end of a route only)

Find information on how to access walks by bus (if available) at the start of each walk description.

Bus timetables can be found at the back of this book.. Please note that timetables are subject to change; check in the Tourist Offices or bus station in **Arrecife** on arrival for up to date information.

Walk descriptions include:

* timing in minutes, shown as (40M)
* compass directions, shown as (NW)
* heights in metres, shown as (1355m)
* GPS waypoints, shown as (Wp.3)

The Canary Islands lie approximately 100 kilometres west of North Africa's Atlantic Coast, and approximately 1100 kilometres south-west of the Spanish Mainland.

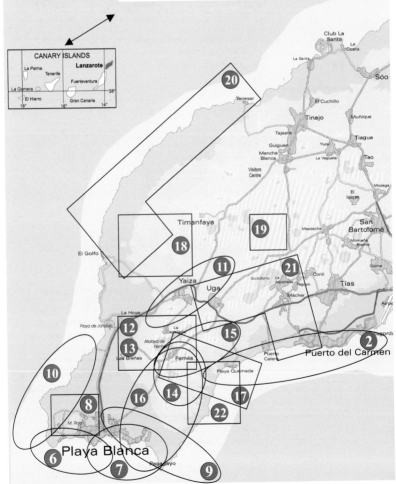

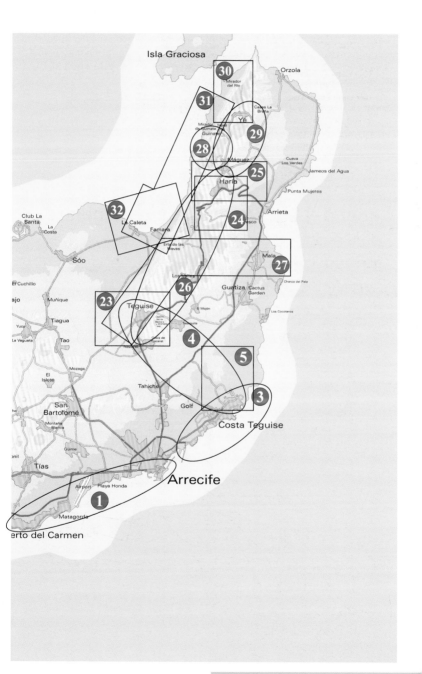

The map sections used in this book have been taken from **Lanzarote Tour & Trail Super-Durable Map** (ISBN 1-899554-95-5) published by Discovery Walking Guides Ltd. All map sections are aligned so that north is at the top of the page. In the interests of clarity, not all waypoints referred to in the walk descriptions are shown in the map sections. Where waypoints positions, but not numbers, are common to two routes, the earlier route's waypoint numbers are shown on the map section.

Lanzarote Tour & Trail Super-Durable Map is a 1:40,000 scale full colour map. For more information on DWG publications, write to DWG Ltd., 10 Tennyson Close, Northampton NN5 7HJ, England, or visit:

www.walking.demon.co.uk   www.dwgwalking.co.uk

Legend-Legende-Leyenda-Légende

ROADS, STRAßE, CARRETERA, ROUTE

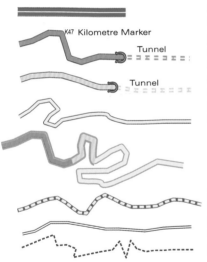

Motorway,
Autobahn, Autopista.

Main road, Haupstraße,
Carretera principal,Route à
grande circulation

Secondary road, Regionalstraße,
Carretera, Route

Minor road, Lokalstraße,
Carretera, Route secondaire

Scenic Driving Routes
Landschaftlich schöne Strecke
Recorrido pintoresco
Parcours pittoresque

Narrow road, Fahrweg,
Camino Rural, Chemin carrosable

Dirt road, Fahrweg,
Camino, Chemin carrosable

Path, Fußweg, Sendero, Sentier

Walking Routes, Wanderweg, Sendero, Chemin.

Walk! Lanzarote Route (Red)   GPS Waypoint
17 see Walk! Lanzarote guide book
Alternative Route (Green)

ALTITUDE, HÖHE, ALTITUD, ALTITUDE

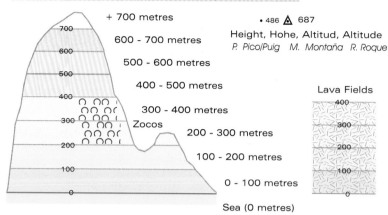

+ 700 metres

600 - 700 metres

500 - 600 metres

400 - 500 metres

300 - 400 metres

Zocos

200 - 300 metres

100 - 200 metres

0 - 100 metres

Sea (0 metres)

• 486 ▲ 687

Height, Hohe, Altitud, Altitude
P. Pico/Puig   M. Montaña   R. Roque

Lava Fields

Lighthouse, Leuchtturm, Faro, Phare 〰 Mirador ᴾ Parking, Parkplatz

Tower, Turm, Torre, Tour ◊ Spring 𝒾 Information ⌂ Hotel Petrol

Church, Kirche, Iglesia, Église Chapel, Kapelle, Ermita, Chapelle

Picnic area, Rastplatz, Zona Recreativa, Pique-nique Golf Course

Cemetery, Friedhof, Cementario, Cimetière ⌨ Bar/Rest

Sports Ground, Sportplatz, Campo deportivo, Terrain de sport

Camping, Campingplatz, Camping, Camping

Wind Turbine, Windkraftwerk, Eólica, Éolienne Urban Area

Commercial Building House Important House Ruin/Barn/Corral

Regional Boundary

The GPS Waypoint lists provided in this **Walk! Lanzarote** guide book by David & Ros Brawn, are as recorded by ourselves during our research of the 32 main walk descriptions contained in the book. In the interests of clarity, not all waypoints included in these lists are shown on the maps which accompany each detailed walk description.

Waypoint Symbols

Where a Waypoint symbol is shown on a map it has been placed alongside the position to which it refers, so as to not obscure the map detail, and is numbered so that it can directly identified against the walk description and waypoint list.

For readers wondering what we are talking about, the GPS Waypoints are also Grid References to the exact locations within each walking route, when used in conjunction with the **Lanzarote Tour & Trail Super-Durable Map**.

All The GPS Waypoints quoted in Walk! Lanzarote, and on the Tour & Trail Map, were recorded during the research of the walking routes, and are subject to the general considerations as to the accuracy of GPS units in the location concerned. Lanzarote has good GPS reception with little, if any, 'mountain shadowing' causing reception problems. Even our Walk 31 'Risco de Famara' route produced a perfect GPS Track, even though much of the route is a long traverse across the massive cliff face. Only in Walk 23 'Teguise - The Ancient Capital' did we have reception problems amongst the buildings, so we have reverted to a 'traditional' description of this historic stroll.

It is virtually impossible to reproduce the exact GPS Waypoint co-ordinates in practice when walking a route. While GPS Waypoints are quoted to 00.0001 minutes of arc, in practice you should expect 10 metres as an acceptable standard of accuracy when you have '3D navigation' (four or more satellites in view); though reception is so good on Lanzarote, that your accuracy will often be closer to 5 metres.

Signal Strength
Signal strength from sufficient satellites is crucial to obtaining an accurate location fix with your GPS unit. In open sky, ridge top, conditions you may have up to 11 satellites in view to give you a GPS location accuracy of 5 metres. Providing you have good batteries, and that you wait until your GPS has full 'satellite acquisition' before starting out, your GPS will perform wonderfully on Lanzarote for all our country routes.

To Input the Waypoints
GPS Waypoint co-ordinates are quoted for the WGS84 datum, used to provide grid references on the Tour & Trail Map, in degrees and minutes of Latitude and Longitude. To input the Waypoints into your GPS we suggest that you:

• Switch on your GPS and select 'simulator' mode.

- Check that your GPS is set to the WGS84 datum (its default datum) and the 'position format' 'hddd° .mm.mmm'.

- Input the GPS Waypoints into a 'route' file with the same number as the walking route number; then when you call up the 'route' on Lanzarote there will be no confusion as to which walking route it refers.

- Repeat the inputting of routes until you have covered all the routes you plan to walk, or until you have used up the memory capacity of your GPS; even the most basic of GPS units will store up to 20 routes of up to 50 Waypoints for each route, and you can always re-programme your GPS while on Lanzarote.

- Turn off your GPS. When you turn the GPS back on it should return to its normal navigation mode.

GPS Waypoints are provided as an additional navigation aid to complement the detailed walk descriptions in Walk! Lanzarote. Knowing exactly where you are in relation to our detailed walk description is a great confidence booster when exploring these new and exciting landscapes. GPS Waypoints are provided for all key navigational points on all walking routes; never again should you find yourself wondering whether you are on the right path or not.

Note that GPS Waypoints complement the detailed walking route descriptions in Walk Lanzarote; and are not intended as an alternative to the detailed walking route description.

Confused by GPS?
If you are confused by talk of GPS, but are interested in how this modern navigational aid could enhance your walking enjoyment, then simply seek out a copy of **GPS The Easy Way**, the UK's best selling GPS manual. Written in an easy to read, lively, style and lavishly illustrated, GPS The Easy Way takes you through all aspects of GPS usage from absolute basics up to GPS Expert and debunking the myths about GPS along the way; an essential purchase for anyone thinking of buying a GPS.

"A compass points north"
but
"A GPS tells you where you are, where you have been, and can show you where you want to go."

"Ask not 'What is GPS?' - ask 'What can GPS do for me?' "

GPS The Easy Way is available from bookshops, outdoor shops, over the internet, and post free from:
Discovery Walking Guides Ltd.
10 Tennyson Close
Northampton NN5 7HJ

www.walking.demon.co.uk & www.dwgwalking.co.uk

From reading the postings on uk.rec.walking internet news group, it is obvious that walkers are very interested in the clothing and equipment used by other walkers. For some this interest borders on obsession, with heated debates over walking poles, boots versus sandals, GPS versus 'map and compass' navigation etc. etc. Walking magazines are packed with clothing and equipment reviews, opinions and adverts, but few walking guide books give more than a cursory mention to recommended clothing and equipment.

Our Walk! Lanzarote walking routes range from strolls around **Teguise** and the coastal promenades (Walks 1, 3, 6,7, 11, and 23) where you might feel distinctly overdressed in more than trainers and casual wear, up to routes where we recommend full walking equipment.

Lanzarote might promote itself as an idyllic holiday destination, but both the climate and the landscape can be extremely harsh. Remorseless sunshine combines with very low (zero) humidity, and a barren rock/lava/grit landscape covers much of the island. Protection against sunburn, sunstroke and dehydration should not be relaxed for even the easiest of routes.

At the risk of upsetting some walking fundamentalists, here is a brief rundown on what we've used on Lanzarote.

BACKPACK

A 25-30 litre day pack should easily cope with all the equipment you think you will need for a day's walking. A design with plenty of outside pockets to give easy access to frequently used items, such as ½litre water bottles, is a good starting point. Well padded straps will spread the load and a waist strap will stop the pack moving about on the more adventurous routes. A ventilated back panel will help clear sweat on hot days and tough routes; a design with a stand-off frame is best for ventilation and worth the small increase in weight. Do spend time adjusting the straps so that you get the most comfortable fit.

As an alternative to traditional backpack designs, you might find the cyclist's packs produced by Nikko (which we use), and similar companies, a good compromise of stand-off frame, capacity, pockets and weight.

FOOTWEAR

While the coastal promenades provide easy strolling, the country walking underfoot conditions range from comfortable dirt tracks to walking trails, and some 'open ground' walking, on rock/lava, usually uneven. Whether you choose boots, shoes or sandals they must be up to the task. You will need a hard sole with plenty of grip and a well padded foot-bed. After wearing my Clarks sandals on the first day, and finding that my walking style was scooping up loads of grit I (David) used a pair of Bestard Race K shoes, worn with thick mountain socks, for all the remaining research. Bestard boots and shoes are not widely available in UK, but if you are on Mallorca call in at their factory shop in Lloseta. Ros completed all the routes in sandals, alternating between her Merrell, Cats and Clarks designs.

Whichever footwear you choose, do make sure that you have covered plenty of kilometres in them before coming to Lanzarote.

SUN PROTECTION

Lanzarote is famous for the intensity of its sunshine. Just look around at the 'booze and snooze' set to see examples of bad sunburn. Wear comfortable loose clothing and always carry a comfortable sun hat. Choose a design that gives you plenty of shade, is comfortable to wear, and stays on your head in windy conditions; our choice are the Rohan 'Legionnaire' style which protects neck and ears. You will be spending several hours a day outdoors and sunburnt ears (and neck) are both painful and embarrassing. Use a high-factor sun cream on all exposed skin.

We favour wrap-round sunglasses which, as well as reducing UV radiation, protect from getting grit in our eyes on windy days, of which Lanzarote has a surplus. When you do take a break sit in the shade and leave the sunburning to the 'booze and snooze' visitors.

WATER & FOOD

Dehydration, like sunburn, is a real danger on Lanzarote, particularly on the longer, more energetic routes. When the sand laden *calima* wind is blowing from the Sahara, humidity drops to zero and the wind leeches moisture from you. In these conditions you might not recognise that you are sweating, because the moisture immediately evaporates.

Always carry as much water as you think you might drink. A couple of ½litre water bottles, a few pence each from local shops, is the minimum, and add extra for routes such as Walks 10, 12, 16, 20, 21, 26, 27, 28, 30 and 31.

Even on shorter routes, we would advise that you carry some survival rations. Rural *tipico* bar/restaurants are mostly designed to cater for the 'coach potato' trade, and survival rations of chocolate bars and the like can provide welcome comfort when out in the wild.

MEDICAL KIT

Antiseptic wipes, antiseptic cream, plasters and bandage are supplemented by lip salve, which can seem like a life saver in Lanzarote's hot dry conditions. Also include tweezers, which you will soon appreciate if you catch a splinter or cactus spine, and a whistle to attract attention if you get into difficulties.

NAVIGATION

Don't compromise - buy the best guide book and the best map, and carry them with you. A compass is useful to orientate yourself at the start of a route and for general directions, but a GPS unit is far more useful - see Using GPS on Lanzarote.

CLOTHING

Choose loose comfortable clothing and add a lightweight jacket to your back pack; Lanzarote is justly famous for sunshine, but we were very grateful for our jackets when pioneering the Walk 15 'Femés Ridge' route; see photos. The island might be mostly desert, but it does rain sometimes so it helps if your lightweight jacket is waterproof.

OTHER EQUIPMENT

You won't want to be carrying excess weight during your walking, especially on the longer routes with major ascents/descents. Digital cameras generally weigh far less than their film equivalents, and a monocular is half the weight of a pair of binoculars. A mobile phone, and money (refreshments, taxis, public telephones, drinks machines etc.) are also recommended.

There are plenty of routes to choose from in Walk! Lanzarote to suit a range of fitness levels and varying in distance from 3 to 22 kilometres and in walking time from 1 hour to the big 6 hour hike of **Femés** to **Playa Blanca**. However, bear in mind that the times given are the actual walking times that we recorded while walking the routes ourselves - you might cover the ground more quickly or slowly. Check your progress against ours early in the walk, and you will soon be able to estimate the time you'll need relative to ours. Also remember that the times given are for continuous walking, so you'll need to add more time for rest stops, picnics, admiring the views, taking photos etc.

If you are new to walking, or out of condition, then we suggest that you choose one of the coastal promenade walks (Walk 1 **Puerto del Carmen** to **Arrecife**, Walk 3 **Costa Teguise**, Walks 6&7, **Playa Blanca**). A couple of other routes will also break you in gently; Walk 19 to **Montaña Cuervo**, or Walk 23 around the old town of **Teguise**. In many cases, there's the choice of a short version of longer or more challenging routes.

To experience the strange volcanic desert landscapes, try Walk 10, on the **Rubicón** plain, or Walk 20 which combines lava fields with the coastline of **Timanfaya**. There are some beautiful beach routes, for example to **Papagayo** on Walk 8, and **Playa del Pozo**, Walk 22. If mountains are more your style, there's the easy **Montaña Roja** one hour route, or Walks 12 to 17 out of **Femés**, taking in the peaks in this beautiful region. And if you thought Lanzarote was lacking in lush vegetation, then the routes in the north of the island, for example Walk 24, 'The Forgotten Trail' or Walk 28 'Helechos Circular', will change your opinion.

Whichever route you choose, read it through a couple of times before setting out, and make sure you have appropriate clothing, equipment and refreshments with you.

SAFETY

- Don't attempt high altitude routes in severe weather. Be prepared to abandon a route and turn back if bad weather closes in.
- Don't walk alone - or at least let someone know where you are planning to walk.
- Wear appropriate clothing and footwear, and carry the right equipment (see Pages 24-26)
- Take frequent drinks of water.
- Shade is scarce on Lanzarote. Protect yourself from the sun.
- Start out early enough - allow plenty of time to complete the route before dark.
- Stay on the route. If it is impassable, retrace your steps.

February 2004 saw the opening of the final sections in a coastal promenade linking **Matagorda** to **Arrecife**, now Lanzarote's longest coastal walkway at over 9 kilometres in length. Some sections are still being worked on as we go to press, but all of the route is open for walkers and strollers. An easy if long route, requiring merely suitable footwear, clothing and sun protection. The beach side bars at **Playa Honda** mean you can conveniently stop for refreshment at the half way stage of the route. If you find 9+ kilometres of walking more than enough, your arrival in **Arrecife** close by the bus terminus makes it easy to catch a **Puerto del Carmen** bus back for your return.

Access by bus:
Take the N°2 **Puerto del Carmen** bus from **Arrecife** and alight at the first stop in **Matagorda**, then walk down past the **Sol Lanzarote Hotel**. From **Puerto del Carmen**, alight at the first stop after the roundabout at the end of the beach road and follow coastal pavement (west, and add 0.7 kilometres) or at the stop by **Sol Lanzarote**.

Access by car:
When you see the **Sol Lanzarote Hotel**, take the road running down the eastern side of the hotel. This is **Calle Agonal** and we've always found plenty of on-street parking, even at weekends.

On foot from **Puerto del Carmen**: Simply walk down to the sea front and follow the beach-side pavement eastwards until meeting our official start. You can walk from the 'old town' on promenade and the beach road pavement, adding 5.5 kilometres and 1 hour to distance and time above.

'Thingy', 12 minutes into the walk

From the end of **Calle Agonal** (Wp1 0M) we follow the broad paved walkway east; this section was once a road, but has now been pedestrianised. We pass a lava tower (lifeguard and red cross station, Wp.2) shortly before coming to the signboard at the start of the new section of walkway (Wp.3 12M) beside a grey rock 'thingy' set in a roundabout at the end of the road.

Now we are striding out, leaving tourism behind, past stone seats set in the lava wall to pass an aerial-bedecked building (Wp.4) before coming to the end of the runway, where the paving is replaced by a boardwalk. This is a popular spot with plane watchers, the big jets making an impressive sight when taking off over us.

Sand swamps the board walk (Wp.5) for a few metres before the way becomes clear again. The boardwalk was chosen for this section so as to protect the 'natural' environment; natural environment next to a very busy runway, now who is kidding who here? The boardwalk seems a bit cheap on construction as we spring along its bouncy surface to pass **Playa de Guasimeta** (Wp.6), a 'cozzie optional' bit of beach, and *zoco* style sunbathing area (Wp.7) to start closing with the **Playa Honda** urbanisation. Eventually the bouncy boardwalk finishes (Wp.8) to be replaced by pebbledash slabs for our welcome arrival at **Bar Mercedes** (Wp.9 45M) facing the impressive sweep of golden sand; if you do miss this refreshment opportunity, there is another at **Bar Mesana** in a few metres.

The second stage of our excursion is along the sea front of **Playa Honda**, again once a road but now more popular as a promenade - except for those owners whose garages face the beach. Our broad walkway twists along the edge of the beach, passing a pair of houses on the seaward side (Wp.11) pre-dating the current planning laws, and a pair of bars (Wp.12) before swinging left to round a crescent of sand. Here, (Wp.13) you can short cut across the sand, though our choice is the easy stroll around the lagoon inside the sand bar, passing another beach entry (Wp.14) before a short climb is followed by steps down to continue on a crude concrete surface. Isn't it funny how the worst section of the promenade fronts the flashiest houses?

Housing ends (Wp.15) as the concrete swings inland and we come onto an unfinished section; hopefully paved by the time you reach here, being easier than our short cut (Wp.16) across the beach past a true beach-house (Wp.17) before coming back onto the official walkway (Wp.18 77M). Back to easy strolling, we leave the sea for a while (Wp.19) to pass inland of **El Cable Yacht Club**. Keeping straight ahead, we go right onto pebbledash slabs and then left to come onto the wide brick paved promenade for our final section into **Arrecife**.

The broad promenade is built directly on the sea front rocks, waves crashing against the wall spraying our route as we are now rapidly closing on the previously distant **Arrecife**. Passing the extensive car park on our left (Wp.21) the neo-classical *Cabildo* building comes into sight on our left along with a large rusty 'thingy'. An easy stroll brings us up to the start of the thematic park, though unfortunately the gardens are in some need of 'TLC', as trees and plants go without water, and the 'ships vents' double as overflowing waste bins; all in all, making for a very shabby entrance to the island's capital. At a 'muse' (Wp.22), which you might mistake for a 'thingy', you can short cut left across the park, though our full route goes on past the 'shipwreck' to the prow (Wp.23 95M) of the 'boat' theme park before swinging left around **Playa Reducto** to meet the road (Wp.24 100M), just to the right of the bus stops. Our choice is to follow the pavement round towards the **Arrecife Gran Hotel** and finish in one of the road side bars.

Arrecife had a rather scruffy air when we were researching in 2004, and closes most religiously for the 13.00 to 16.00 siesta; about the time you are likely to arrive. If you do arrive during opening hours, then head for the pedestrianised shopping streets where modern shops jostle with establishments more often seen in 'Are you being served?' and 'Open all hours', which they certainly are not.

2. COASTAL DISCOVERY

Lanzarote's southern coast provides a popular walking route from **Puerto del Carmen** to the new resort and marina of **Puerto Calero**, an easy stroll. We continue on past **Puerto Calero** to reach **Playa Quemada**, a rather scruffy coastal village but graced by *tipico* bar/restaurants.

The walking is easy rather than spectacular, but the route provides a good introduction to the island's countryside. Ideal as a stroll out, taking a drink in the new marina before continuing on to **Playa Quemada** for a relaxed lunch. Repeat the procedure on the way back for a very laid back day's walking.

It is unusual for us to congratulate a coastal development for actually improving a walking route, but in this case the new coastal promenade at **Puerto Calero** has tidied up what was once a picky part of our route.

> **Short Walk**
> To **Puerto Calero** marina and return (2 hours, 9 kilometres)

We start out from the old port at the western end of **Puerto del Carmen** (Wp.1 0M) by taking the steps up by the **El Veradero** to **Calle Los Infantes**, at the end of which, by the **Rincón** apartments, we go up the stair with a rope handrail to come onto the start of the coastal walkway (Wp.2). It's an unpromising start as we climb up a steep rock bluff, which brings us onto a broad pavement which runs along below villas. Now it is easy strolling above the sea until the paving ends (Wp.3), replaced by a wide dirt path as we pass the end of the inland wall at a flight of steps (Wp.4 15M).

Here, the path narrows to normal width as it continues to a tiny *barranco*; either clamber down the metre drop, or swing right in a loop - both options rejoin across the depression. Our route runs out into a flat barren landscape dotted with squat walled villas as the path comes back to the cliffs. We pass a couple of pretty cliff side villas before coming to the lava-walled villas at the entrance to **Barranco de Quiquere**, a veritable oasis when set against this barren landscape. Passing the villas on the seaward side, we walk above a sunbathing area accessed by steps and handrails as our route swings right following the *barranco*. We come up between the lava wall and the *barranco* to come onto the end of a tarmac lane by the villa's entrance (Wp.5 32M).

If this is your first southern walk, then you should allow yourself the luxury of taking in the distant views. Inland, the central massif finishes at the pass to **La Geria**, and the large building set on the final ridge is a *parapente* launch point. Depending on the winds, you might see whole flocks of these colourful fragile fliers gliding down to their landing strip inland from **Puerto Calero**.

To the right of the pass is the 'pencil-point' peak of **Montaña de Guardilama**, which offers Lanzarote's most spectacular viewpoint to those fit enough to brave the ascent; our **La Geria** route offers the opportunity to experience those lofty delights.

Ahead are the misty southern mountains which rise almost sheer from the **Rubicón** plain. The antennaed peak of **Atalaya de Femés** sits above the pretty village of **Femés**, our centre for some adventurous walking routes amongst the peaks and *barrancos* of this little-known region. Yes, there is plenty of exciting walking ahead of you.

You could cross the **Barranco de Quiquere** by descending to the sunbathing area, crossing the *barranco* floor and scrambling up the rocks before struggling round the seaward walls of the villas in order to rejoin the coastal path. But this is a relaxed route, so we take the more civilised option of following the tarmac lane inland to a track going left (Wp.6) accessing a number of villas. A short climb takes us up and around the villas to resume the coastal walk.

Our route takes us along low cliffs set above a lava plateau foreshore before dropping into a small *barranco*. Once out of the *barranco*, we join a dirt track heading for **Puerto Calero**, which is now of course much closer. This barren region has been used by quad bikers, resulting in a proliferation of tracks; if in any doubt, keep heading for the marina on the most suitable track/trail. It's an

easy stroll, so long as there are no pesky quad bikers about, as we come up to overlook the marina (Wp.7), but this is a case of so near but so far; do not be tempted by paths appearing to drop into the marina, as they only run up against a big lava wall! Follow the main track inland to reach the **Puerto Calero** road by the roundabout (Wp.8). Going left (E), we walk along to the main crossroads, turning downhill for a skittering descent into the marina, noting the **Paseo Maritimo** walkway on our right just before the marina entrance (58M).

Puerto Calero marina

For our continuation on to **Playa Quemada**, we take the **Paseo Maritimo** (Wp.9 0M) from beside the marina entrance. We follow this wide elegant walkway as it undulates along out past the marina, there are a number of stairs giving access down to the foreshore before the walkway turns inland up to a T-junction (Wp.10 10M) at the **Hotel Hespería**.

Although it looks like a dead end we go left (W) to walk past the restaurant entrance onto a small rock headland with marine rope railing. We follow the rope down steps to cross a tiny artificial beach and climb a rock stairway that brings us up to the western end of the hotel (Wp.11) from where we come inland beside the hotel to pick up a track (Wp.12) that curves up over the next headland.

The rock stairway

The dusty track takes us into an undulating landscape. Staying on the track, we head towards the coast. This is another area used by quadbikers resulting in a myriad of tracks and trails. To avoid confusion, keep to the coastal track/trail as we go through a series of gentle ascents and descents to head westwards across small hills and shallow valleys; when a track turns inland a walking trail links us to the next track section. Only when we walk up a longer than usual slope do we come into view of the first houses of **Playa Quemada**; this point (Wp.13) is grandly shown as a trig point of 22 metres on military maps, but is hardly noticeable on the ground.

Following the track, we come to the first houses, the track becoming tarmac for an easy stroll down the first street to a small square, then it is downhill past the beach front houses to a restaurant (Wp.14 32M) where you could walk down the beach front instead of the road. Cutting through to the beach we stroll along to the end of the houses to come onto the tarmac as it heads inland to the **7 Islas** and **La Casita** bar/restaurants. Sitting on one of these terraces and taking refreshment, we can absorb the charm of this informal settlement of small houses and weekender homes. Some might describe its informal style as scruffy, but there is no doubting its quaintness. Take your time relaxing before returning to the resort by your outward route.

3. COASTAL PROMENADE - COSTA TEGUISE

The massive **Barceló Suites Hotel** complex dominates our approach into **Costa Teguise** and rather sets the tone for the resort in looking somewhat well used and being some distance from the sea. In **Playa Blanca** and **Puerto del Carmen** most of the tourist accommodation is strung out along the sea front, but **Costa Teguise** has opted to push inland and mixes tourist and residential developments, which means that you could be staying some distance from the sea during a holiday here.

As with **Playa Blanca**, both ends of the coastal promenade are somewhat isolated, so our route finishes with an inland section to take us to the nearest taxi rank and bus stop. You can easily short cut the final section of the route, as our short walk alternative.

Short Walk
At **Playa Cucharas**, turn inland at Wp.10 into the commercial centre and turn right on its inland side, for the short step to our taxi rank finish (4 kilometres).

Access by bus: Nº1 and within **Costa Teguise**: Simply walk towards the sea and start wherever you strike the Coastal Promenade.

Access by Car: On street car parking at the western end of the promenade and along the resort's main access road, plus commercial centre's car parks.

We start at the western end of the promenade on the turning circle at the end of **Calle los Volcanes** (Wp.1 0M); plenty of on-street car parking despite the development taking place.

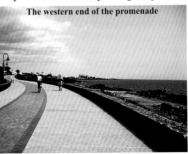

The western end of the promenade

Taking to the broad, brick paved, promenade we head east between the lava rock foreshore and smug seafront villas until we come to the stark seaward face of the **Las Coronas Hotel** (Wp.2), which has attracted the local graffiti artists, facing a rather poor piece of beach.

We pass on to the much more inviting **Playa Bastián** (Wp.3) where a paved walkway gives access into the resort, just before we pass a lifeguard/red cross station 'martello' tower (Wp.4 14M) and pass inland of the **Villa Toldeo Bar/rest** to come to a pedestrian roundabout (Wp.5).

Ahead, a grit track leads into the resort's commercial centre as we keep right to pass to seaward of an ugly abandoned development and then **Punta**

Playa Ancla

Jabillo, hotel left and then beach right, marked by a fake windmill (Wp.6). Round the beach, we pass the **Neptuno** commercial centre and car parks before coming to the second windmill (Wp.7 25M) opposite the **Nautilus** apartments. The brick-paved promenade now changes to eroded pebbledash slabs, as we walk between the lava foreshore and a disused building site to round the point and come to the sight of two tall 'thingies' which dominate the bay.

One of Costa Teguise's 'windmills'

We are heading towards the resort's main beach of **Playa Cucharas**, as we come to cross the dock's access road at a roundabout (Wp.8); There are actually three 'thingies'at the end of the dock, two tall and one squat, their redundant decayed appearance rather summing up this section of resort.

The scene is one of a pleasant beach fronted by crass commercialism combined with urban decay as we walk past another decayed 'thingy' and abandoned commercial premises before hitting a clutch of Brit and Irish bars, including the imaginatively named **The Sunburnt Arms**, catering for the volume tourist. A short flight of steps (Wp.9) takes us up across a bar terrace to swing right in front of the scruffiest piece of seafront un-development so far. Things improve - they could hardly get worse - as we come to the access roads and bars on our left and overlarge plumbing fixtures on our right; as a collection they possibly rank as a 'thingy'. At a junction (Wp.10 41M) a path goes straight ahead, our Short Walk option to cut inland and climb up to the

Cucharas commercial centre, while we go right to walk around the final section of **Playa Cucharas** where the promenade devolves into rock and sand.

Across the sand, we pass the last breakwater (Wp.11) at the end of the beach to continue on a rough track between low dunes and the lava foreshore, the way lined with very old rope handrail fencing, to come onto the end of an old road (Wp.12 49M) by a breakwater. We come back towards the resort and the pebbledash slabbed continuation of the promenade to start curving around **Playa de los Charcos**. These are much classier developments than around **Playa Cucharas**, as we pass the fake windmill (Wp.13 52M) beside an inland lagoon which is part of the **Sands Beach Villas** development, known in a previous life as **Lanzarote Beach Club**.

Passing the breakwater enclosing the beach we come to the end of **Sands Villas**, and the end of civilisation as **Costa Teguise** knows it, to walk past an original windmill dating from the sea salt era. The promenade, now rough concrete, passes a bleak, fenced building site and finishes just before a sea front house (Wp.14). We head inland alongside the fenced site on a dirt road, passing a track off to more distant houses before coming onto the **Avenida de las Islas** street (Wp.15 63M). Heading left (W) we walk along the pavement back towards civilisation, now passing **Sands Beach Villas** inland facade. A Taxi rank is our official finishing point (a 4 euro ride back to our start point if you do not want to walk), but you will probably want to follow our example of continuing to **Cucharas** commercial centre (Wp.16 74M) where behind the shabby facade you will find some decent cafés facing seawards, for some well-earned refreshment.

4. SUNDAY MARKET SPECIAL - CAMINO EL CHARCO

With the advent of the car, many of Lanzarote's commerce routes were upgraded from donkey trails to tarmac roads. When Lanzarote was first colonised, pirate raids dictated establishing the capital at **Teguise**, protected by the **Castillo de Santa Bárbara**. From here routes ran down to the coast; one passing through the small settlement of **Teseguite** and then straight down to **Salinas El Charco**. Refrigeration largely killed the sea salt market, but this old donkey trail route is still shown on some maps. This is one old route which still survives, though the new **Tahiche-Mala** road necessitates a short diversion through a tunnel.

Sunday is the day to walk this route using a 'market special' bus, seeing the island's busiest street market before setting out on the old 'salt trail'.

Access by bus: Sunday market specials go from **Costa Teguise** (Nº11), **Puerto del Carmen** (Nº12), and **Playa Blanca** (Nº13).

> **Short Walk**
> To **Castillo de Santa Bárbara** and return, (ascents/descents 110 metres).

Our starting point is at the start of the access road to **Castillo de Santa Bárbara** (Wp.1 0M). If you are coming from the market, then make your way to the main road, cross over and walk up the pavement to reach our 'official' start. With the old castle above us we have a slogging ascent up the tarmac

(SE) between storm-water eroded earth banks. As we ascend we are looking for a faint dirt track leaving the tarmac (Wp.2) which comes just before the road gets even steeper.

...views open up over Teseguite ...

Gratefully, we leave the steepening tarmac to stroll along the narrow track between stone walls as it contours around the hill to come to cultivated fields contrasting with the generally barren landscape. Views open up over **Teseguite** and down to the coast as our track goes right to go around another area of storm-water eroded earth banks.

Keeping to the main track (Wp.3) we swing left towards **Teseguite** to stroll gently downhill with extensive views expanding over the valley and up to the **Ermita de las Nieves** and radomes of Walk 26. Our track swings downhill through the sunburnt landscape to bring us onto a tarmac street (Wp.4) and the first houses of **Teseguite**.

Teseguite might be a small settlement, but it can be confusing to navigate to find our exit route. Going left, we stroll down (NNE) to the second junction (Wp.5) marked by a 'palm tree' roundabout outside the cemetry, where we go right (E). We stroll gently downhill to cross over a village street, and pass **Casarino** on our right before coming to the next crossroads (Wp.6), where we go left (E). It is downhill again to a T-junction (Wp.7) at the end of **Calle Revuelta**, where we go left and immediately right on **Calle Cadina** to come along to another T-junction (Wp.8). Here we go right to start our exit into the country. At a junction (Wp.9) with 'Finca Luna' signed left, we go right, and where the tarmac lane swings right, we go straight ahead on a dirt track (Wp.10), the **Camino El Charco** - well, we did warn you it could be confusing.

We head out into the country between stone walls, passing a troglodyte style hut (Wp.11) to come into an area littered by a 'rain of stones'. It's downhill on the faint track, and after it swings left and right views open up across the sloping plain to **Montaña Corona** with **Costa Teguise** peeking round its base. Water erosion has washed away sections of the track as cultivated fields start on our left, just before the track runs out at a triangular field (Wp.12).

To find our onward route we go right across the edge of the field to go through a gap in a 'pile of stones' wall to find a faint trail heading down towards **Montaña Corona** along a gully. We pick our way down the shallow gully between fields to come out into the open; ahead a pair of cultivated fields stands out in the barren landscape. Keeping the water runoff on our right, we are back to easy strolling, our trail crossing the runoff (Wp.13) and becoming better defined as we come to the cultivated fields. Now we simply keep

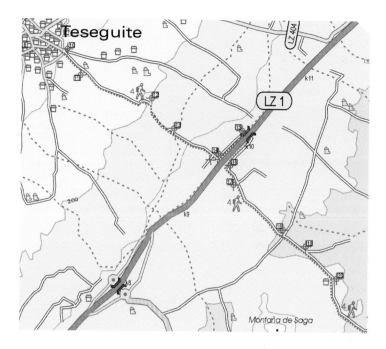

straight ahead on the track, passing a pylon and then a 'bedstead' gated property on our right where the track becomes more used, to come down to meet the old main road (Wp.14/.

Originally our route went straight across the old main road, but the new road is wider, faster and busier. To avoid any risk we go left (NE) on the old road to a tunnel under the new road (Wp.15) where we come onto remains of the old road. Going right, we continue alongside the new road on a track to come back to the line of the **Camino El Charco** (Wp.16/. Obstacle passed, we are back to simple navigation as we follow a track heading towards **Montaña Corona** (SSE) and the coast, passing a minor track off to our left (Wp.17) and a pair of ruins before topping a rise where our track runs down to cultivated fields and a crossroads of tracks (Wp.18).

Coming down to the crossroads from the new road it is very noticeable how the land has changed. Above the main road the land is cheerfully barren, but below, it's as if this forgotten plain is cowering beneath the dominant heights of **Caldera** and **Tahiche**. Grey is the dominant colour, relieved a little by the spiny grey-green Lanzarote Fire Bush (Launaea arborescens) which dominates the long-abandoned fields in this harsh landscape.

At least it is easy walking, passing a minor track (Wp.19) as we come gently uphill past cultivated fields to the unexpected sight of a house. Passing the house (Wp.20) and then another track off left to a field, we walk alongside a stone wall to come over a small rise; views open up to the ocean, though **Costa Teguise** is hidden behind the bulk of **Montaña Corona**. We drop down to cross a water runoff (Wp.21) where a faint track goes straight ahead, while our track swings right.

Approaching Costa Teguise

It's a featureless *malpais* littered with stones, our track changing to a more comfortable sand base as we curve towards **Costa Teguise**. An easy stroll brings us back onto the *malpais* at a small rise which brings the sea and **Costa Teguise** into view.

Our track becomes fainter as we cross a small water runoff (Wp.22) and then come up to see our faint track running across towards the **Hotel Beatrix** reception. The track gets even rougher as we pick our way down to step gratefully onto the pavement (Wp.23) outside this large hotel.

While **Playa Blanca** has its **Montaña Roja**, **Costa Teguise** has **Montaña Corona**. Although the peaks differ by only 30 metres altitude, their natures are quite different. **Corona** might only be 231 metres high, but it is quite a tricky peak with a steep, pathless, final ascent and a slippery, shale-covered path descent. These two sections are joined by a ridge top walk around the rim of the *caldera* which might upset vertigo sufferers, and certainly should not be attempted in windy weather.

Those are the bad points, but for experienced walkers the views from the top fully justify the difficult ascent, and the ridge top walk is a pleasure for the confident. In windy weather, and for anyone unsure of tackling the ascent/ridge/descent, we have a low level short walk option suitable for all.

Access by car: Park on the road past the massive **Hotel Beatriz** before the road swings left.

Access by bus: From the most easterly bus stop on the Nº1 route, take pavements approximately NW to the **Hotel Beatriz**.

> **Short Walk**
> Follow main route to the trail crossroads at Wp.7, then turn right to follow the lower trail as it contours around the *caldera* to the trail crossroads at Wp.13; then resume the main route.

Starting out on the western pavement (Wp.1 0M), we walk away from the resort, a ruin ahead of us on a small spur as the road and pavement swing left to climb past a pretty valley on our right, contrasting with the harsh *malpais* elsewhere. The spiny aulaga or Lanzarote firebush (Launaea arborescens) and saltbush (Suaeda vermiculata) invade the pavement, slowly returning this failed urbanisation back to nature, as we swing right to walk through the largely barren *malpais* in a gentle ascent. On this uninteresting section even an old electricity junction box (Wp.2) merits a mention as we head toward the mountain. Our pavement climbs up to a crest, and as it curves left we step off onto a jeep track (Wp.3 14M).

The track runs across open ground toward a gap in a stone wall. Passing a small trail off to our right (Wp.4), we climb up to the gap (Wp.5 20M) to find two large stone cairns which mark the trail to the base of **Montaña Corona**. It is easy walking along the trail to pass a large cairn (Wp.6) and stone designs, better seen from the peak, to arrive at a crossroads of trails (Wp.7 24M).

Our trail stands out clearly ahead.

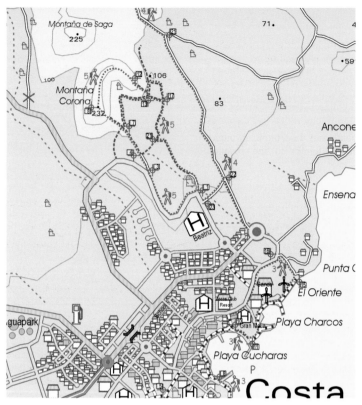

For our Short Walk, turn right here and follow the trail round the *caldera* to the large stone cairn on a spur (Wp.13); this is part of Landscapes ascent route which has arrived at this crossroads from the west.

Montaña Corona looks both big and steep from this viewpoint, so girding our loins we set off up the lower slope on the stony trail, easier as an ascent than descent. The trail zigzags, more for artistic reasons than for any practical use, as we take frequent stops on this 'puff and grunt' climb. Our path disappears as we come onto bedrock, those stone designs by the crossroads much clearer from this elevated position. Our ascent is not vertiginous in the normal sense, but is developing into a steep almost scrambling climb; face the slope not the views when taking a break. We come slowly up past small volcanic blowholes, heading for the highest point above us, until finally we come up onto the summit of **Montaña Corona** (Wp.8 50M).

After that slightly unnerving climb, we gratefully take in the extensive views. Although we are only at 231 metres altitude, the low plains give the impression of a much higher altitude. Thoughtfully the rocks on the summit make for comfortable seating allowing us to enjoy a break before tackling the descent.

From the high point our return route is along the rock ridge of the *caldera*, a far more comfortable open ground route than our earlier ascent. We set off, picking our way carefully over the rocks and edge round a large boulder (Wp.9); this is definitely a 'Stop, and look at the view' section of the route.

Montaña de Saga is a beautiful cone of reds and browns to the north of us as we cross a broad rock cap to the ridge (Wp.10) before negotiating a trench through the ridge by caves (Wp.11). We are now curving south and descending through rough terrain to the second height point (Wp.12 62M).

... Montaña de Saga is a beautiful cone of reds and browns ...

A grit/shale path leads straight down the slope towards the large stone cairn on the saddle below, the path zigzagging as it loses height but this is still a very picky, slippery descent before arriving at the crossroads of trails (Wp.13 78M) just above the big stone cairn; our short walk option (and Landscapes) arriving here from the west.

Most walkers now plunge past the cairn and down the slippery, picky, loose shale trail to the flood plain fifty metres below, but if like us you have had enough of uncomfortable descents then we have a slightly longer but much more civilised alternative. From the crossroads we go left (N) on a narrow trail which curves round the mountain to a faint path junction (Wp.14 81M) where we keep right to descend amongst the foothills as our trail curves towards the resort. A faint trail (Wp.15) goes onto a low rise as we continue down the small valley to cross its water runoff (Wp.16), where our trail is reduced to a trace crossing the flood plain towards a small cairn of stones (Wp.17 89M) where we meet the main path.

There are traces of paths almost everywhere on the flood plain, and the low ridges and big mountain offer no navigational sighting points; just the sort of country where GPS waypoint (or PNF) navigation scores highly. From the cairn we follow the sandy trail (SSW) to a junction (Wp.18) where we go right and then a path joins us from the left (Wp.19), shortly followed by a path off to our right (Wp.20). We keep straight on the main path to close with old stone walls lining the valley, where we start climbing gently up past terraces abandoned millennia ago; do not pay any attention to white painted supposed cairns, as these are land boundary markers. Despite carrying Alan's route on a second GPS we disbelieve the faint path going up by a wall to climb up onto a low ridge (Wp.21 99M) where **Costa Teguise** comes into view.

Ahead a path runs across to the wall (Wp.4 on our outward route) while we go left on a fainter trail to meet a stone wall (Wp. 22) where we swing right (S) to head towards the **Hotel Beatriz**. Our trail heads down beside a stone wall, getting stonier underfoot as we head for the ruin seen at the start of our walk. We come down to a corner of the stone walled field (sic) to take a path (Wp.23) which comes down onto a clearer trail (Wp.24) which follows a small stony valley. Our path widens to a track passing a path on our left (Wp.25) as the valley flattens out and our car comes into view ahead and we curve away from the water runoff to come back onto the pavement beside our start point (112M) at the end of our compact adventure.

6. COASTAL PROMENADE - PLAYA BLANCA WEST

Playa Blanca is Lanzarote's newest and showiest resort, but it is a resort of two halves, so for our first exploration we will test out the affluent western promenade. It's easy strolling on a paved promenade, although it would seriously benefit from a *tipico* bar at its end on the edge of the **Rubicón** desert.

Access by Bus
Take bus N°6, alight at the port bus stop, and walk down to the blue bar on the right where the coastal promenade starts.

Access by Car
Park either opposite the **Centro Commercial Limones** or around the port area.

We start out on the promenade (Wp1 0M) to walk alongside bars on the seaward face of the commercial centre; now with a much smarter appearance than in the days before the promenade opened. The port slips behind us as the brick-paved walkway runs along the top of cliffs and curves right around the **Lanzarote Park Hotel** (Wp.2) and comes down to the beach and bars in front of **Playa Flamingo**. From the end of the beach we climb up to a viewpoint (Wp.3 15M) manufactured out of an old gun pit.

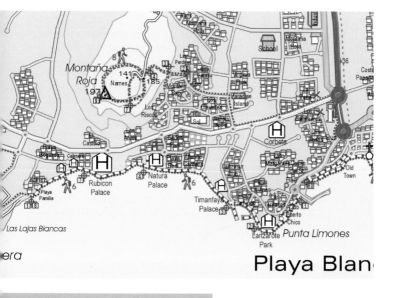

After the small climb it is up and down past the **Timanfaya Palace Hotel**, and its mini beach, then it is past the new development of **Playa Real**, to stroll past the seaward visage of the **Natura Palace Hotel**. At the end of the **Natura Palace** is a walkway (Wp.4 28M) up to the road serving the hotel, an alternative return route on pavements.

A cute wooded bridge (Wp.5) takes us over a water runoff to start passing the extensive grounds of the **Rubicón Palace Hotel**; almost a town in itself, if the size of its jacuzzi (Wp.6) is anything to go by. By comparison the seaward face of the **Calimera** activity hotel (Wp.7) is a fussy collection of little *zocos* and tiny beaches festooned with 'hotel residents only' signs.

Putting the fussiness behind us we pass another hotel before reaching **Playa Familia** artificial beach in front of the **Kamezi** villas, where the promenade finishes at the end of the villa development (Wp.8 44M). Looking round the development wall, you find the **Rubicón** desert and battle-scarred lighthouse, a direct contrast to our manicured promenade.

Montaña Roja stands out ahead.

Now, if only someone had built a cliff-top bar at this point, it would be the perfect easy stroll. We return by retracing our outward route along the promenade and back to the port.

7. COASTAL PROMENADE - PLAYA BLANCA EAST

You might think that one resort's two coastal promenades are going to be roughly similar, but not in Playa Blanca. While the western promenade has the v-v-vroom of booming tourism, the eastern arm suffers from the putt-putt of an old moped, and once past the impressive **Rubicón Marina** and **Volcán Lanzarote Hotel** we are into a patchwork development where sections of promenade are linked by dirt paths.

Our choice is to drive to the far end and walk into **Playa Blanca** 'old town'. That way, your refreshment opportunities are improving all the time, and you have the option of a taxi back to your start if you don't feel like walking; starting out from the 'old town' is the exact opposite!

Access by Bus
If not staying in **Playa Blanca**, take the N°6 bus and alight at the second roundabout, and walk down the road to a third roundabout, where walkways go down to link to the coastal promenade. Your route is as described below but in reverse.

Access by Car
Follow the road down through the third roundabout and head west. After a junction signed to **Rubicón Marina**, take a right at the next roundabout to drive down and park in the cul-de-sac by the **Iberostar Papagayo Hotel**. The

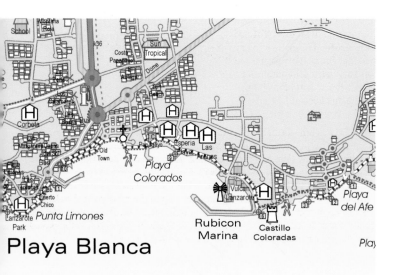

promenade is at the end of the cul-de-sac, and its start is 150 metres away eastwards.

The eastern promenade finishes at the **Playa del Afe** (Wp.1 0M), a once-popular cozzie- optional pebble beach before development arrived. Note that although the 'Playa Papagayo' blue sign points inland, the traditional walking route to this beautiful beach is across **Playa del Afe** to paths leading up the head land on the seaward side of the **Papagayo Arena Hotel**.

From the end of the promenade, we head up past the **Iberostar Papagayo Hotel** to the cul-de-sac on our right (Wp.2) to continue past the **Las Moreras** houses and to the end of this section of promenade (Wp.3). Going right, we cross a turning circle onto a dirt trail heading between the inland developments and the grandly named little martello tower of **Castillo Coloradas** to pass two road accesses (Wp.4 & Wp.5), from where we can see on our right an unusual phenomenon; a man-made imitation volcanic slag heap! Continuing on the trail past the houses, we come to a T-junction on a rock-laid walkway overlooking the **Rubicón Marina** (Wp.6 12M).

Down the steps (right), or slopes (left), we have a choice of following the paved walkway (our GPS track), or making our way through the sizeable but unoccupied (when were last there) marina.

Whether you agree with the grafitti proclaiming that these are 'concrete monuments to Mammon that have ruined a natural coastline' or an impressive development bringing Lanzarote into the modern age, you have to agree that the marina and the 'Portmeirion-esque' **Volcán Lanzarote Hotel** are very striking. From the marina, we can see that the imitation slag heap is in fact part of the hotel's architectural design!

The Rubicón Marina

From the western side of the marina's access road we come back onto seafront promenade (Wp.7) to continue alongside the lava foreshore, passing a house engulfed in trees (Wp.8) before coming back to hotel developments. The promenade twists down to pass **Playa Coloradas** beach (Wp.9) and then climbs to bring the 'old town' into view. For the final stage, we are squeezed between bars and the sea, passing stairways up to the main road should you wish to escape at any time. Keeping straight ahead on the promenade we finally leave the bars behind as we come to overlook the port and the paved walkway swings right to take us up to the road (Wp.10 60M).

8. MONTAÑA ROJA

197 metres might not sound like much of a mountain, but in its location in the flat deserts of **Playa Blanca**, this counts as a high summit. Easy way finding on well marked paths with enough of a climb for a sense of achievement, this is a very popular ascent; perhaps because it is such a contrast to the featureless resort development. A very popular route with all ages, we were accompanied by a three year old boy and his parents on our latest visit.

Short Walk option - this *is* the short walk.

If arriving by bus (Nº6), add 2½ kilometres each way from the bus station to our official start at Wp.1.

If you are driving, we suggest parking at the outer fringes of the development, but should you be arriving by bus you have the dubious pleasure of quite a long walk through the urban sprawl.

Starting from the new bus station we head inland (N) along the main road to pass the CEPSA petrol station and go left (W) at the roundabout. We have an easy stroll along the **Avenida Faro Pechiguera** pavement until we come to the second roundabout where we go right (N) to come gently uphill to the **Paradise Island Club**, where we turn left (W) onto **Avenida Noruega**.

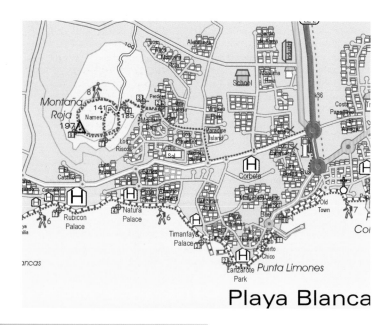

Our ascent of Montaña Roja lies ahead.

At last we are heading for the mountain, passing **Los Clavelles** on our left as we head uphill to the road junction alongside **Montaña Baja** development; drivers should park on the road in this general area.

The 'Al Volcan' sign (Wp.1 0M) points us up the road, to turn off and onto the popular walking trail (Wp.2) which heads up the mountain. It is a dusty sloping path which winds its way up towards the ridge, passing a path coming from the left (Wp.3, and an alternative start route), for us to come onto the broad back of the ridge (Wp.4 15M) to meet a dirt road coming in from the north.

Stone names decorate the floor of the *caldera*.

Our choice is to go left to circle the crater clockwise, gently uphill overlooking a large array of 'stone names' which have been laid out on the floor of the *caldera*.

Following our ascent, we now have an easy stroll with views over the new hotels to **Papagayo** (Wp.5). At a path junction (Wp.6) we have an optional peak to visit on our left, or can go down to a saddle (Wp.7) where a path descends into the *caldera*; an optional steep short cut. Continuing round the crater rim we have a climbing section alongside lichen-covered rocks to a saddle viewpoint (Wp.8) and then a moderately serious ascent up to the trig point (Wp.9 27M). After the trig point we pass another saddle viewpoint (Wp.10), after which our trail descends, curving right and flattening out for an easy stroll along to the dirt track (Wp.11) into the *caldera*. Now it is gently up to meet our upward path (Wp.4 40M) on the wide ridge, and back down the dusty trail to our car - or if using the bus, a much longer stroll back into the resort.

9. PAPAGAYO BEACH

Playa de Papagayo is one of the most photographed locations on Lanzarote, and in our view the one that truly lives up to its image when you arrive there. The easy option is to drive there, following the road signs onto the dirt roads on the southern **Rubicón Plain**, pay your 'gate' fee and park in the extensive parking area near the bars; you are then left with only the steep descent to, and ascent from, this cliff-enclosed perfect beach.

The easy 'car' option is eschewed by aficionados like us, who feel that the beauty of the beaches in this isolated region is enhanced by expending a bit of effort in gaining the reward. **Playa Mujeres** and **Pozo**, which we cross on the way to **Papagayo**, and **Playa Congrio** are also beautiful beaches with the added attraction of being cozzie-optional. So to make a day of it, take your cozzie - or not, as the mood takes you - and enjoy the best beaches on the island, their beauty enhanced by the barren surroundings in which they are found.

Access by Bus
Alight from the Nº6 bus at the roundabout after the petrol station, and walk down into the 'old town' to join the Extended Walk.

Access by Car
On the LZ2, go straight over the petrol station roundabout and the next roundabout to a third roundabout at the edge of the old town. Here, go left (there is no other way) to head east on **Avenida Papagayo**, keeping on the main road until you encounter blue (walker) **Playa Papagayo** signs; yellow signs will direct on the dirt road and 'gate' route for drivers. When you see the sign directing walkers onto a cinder track, blocked to vehicle access by large boulders, look for an on-street parking place on the road up to the **Papagayo Arena Hotel**.

Short Walk
To **Playa Mujeres** and return.

Extended Walk
Take Walk 7, Coastal Promenade - Playa Blanca East f rom the 'old town' to the start of this route and return the same way. When you reach the end of the last stretch of coastal promenade blue signs direct you inland to our official start point, but you could cross the shingle beach to paths that climb up the headland on the hotel's seaward side; see map section.

So many people have walked this route over the years, in all its possible forms, that we have literally a confusion of tracks and trails, most of which will eventually lead you to **Papagayo**; for a description we could simply say "Go east into the wilderness, and stop when you find paradise", but you probably expect a bit more than that. For GPS users, loading up our waypoints will be a great help, while PNF users with both track and waypoints will consider wayfinding a doddle. For those without the benefit of satellite technology, do follow our outward route; it may not always be the best, but it's the way we arrived at paradise.

We start out from the street below the **Papagayo Arena Hotel** where a blue 'Playa Papagayo' sign (Wp.1 0M) directs us up a cinder track. Past the boulders barring vehicle access, we climb up to a junction (Wp.2) behind the hotel and take the faint track to the left to come up onto a featureless desert plateau - featureless except for the pointless trig point on our front left that supposedly marks the peak of **Papagayo**, but do not be drawn towards it.

Keeping to the faint track we come up a rise that brings the beaches into view, car windscreens acting like mirrors in the large car parks as our route curves right past a cairn to a faint junction (Wp.3) where we keep straight on towards the distant car park. Strolling over the headland, we have various trails on our right as we come to the top of a steep trail (Wp.4) which gives us a skittery descent down to the back of **Playa Mujeres (**Wp.5 16M) beside the first car park.

Walking across the rear of the beach behind the dunes, we pass the second car park (Wp.6) to a choice of a steep sandy path which runs up from the beach, or we can continue ahead up a sandy *barranco*, followed by an open-ground ascent over rock onto the next headland - our choice.

Cairns provide approximate direction markers to the start of a path (Wp.7) dropping down to **Playa del Pozo**, the path finishing in a small rock scramble to drop us onto the beach (Wp.8/30M).

Straight across the beach, we head for a path (Wp.9) climbing the sloping rock face onto the next headland. We climb up the path, the sand changing to purple rock as we come onto the headland, the car park now much closer as we cross

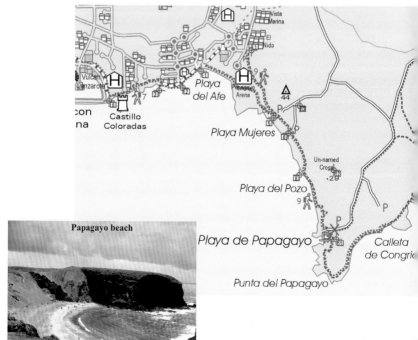

Papagayo beach

a water-eroded gully (Wp.10) followed by an ascent, and crossing a second gully before coming up to the bars above **Papagayo** beach (Wp.11 45M).

Past the bar's generator, a manicured walkway is signed to the beach taking us between the bars. There's a choice of three bars for refreshments and ,given their spectacularly isolated position, prices are very reasonable; regard a refreshment stop on their terrace as compulsory, and enjoy the views down onto Lanzarote's best beach. If you are planning on sunbathing, take one of the steep paths which lead down to the perfect beach, though take care on their slippery surfaces, and it will be (of course) an equally steep climb back up.

Playa Mujeres behind us on the return.

For our return we chose an inland wandering route from the car park, crossing those gullies higher up (much easier to cross) and taking in the wooden cross (Wp.12) and line of boulders before meeting the access track to **Playa Mujeres** at its junction (Wp.13) before rejoining our outward route at Wp.5.

There are so many tracks and trails through this desert landscape that you could navigate back by simply heading north and avoiding any pitfalls. If you do not have a compass or GPS, then use the trig point pillar as your general direction marker.

10. PEÑA DEL RUBICÓN

Deserts have a strange unreality all of their own. Driving across the **Rubicón** desert, it appears that nothing has happened here in aeons, and walking there gives an even greater sense of timelessness; it's easy to imagine that whole civilisations might have disappeared under the wastes of the world's great deserts. Our excursion is along the seaward margin of the **Rubicón**, passing some beautiful rock pools set in the lava foreshore, to the 'peña' of this desert, the long abandoned **Atlante del Sol Hotel**, a monument to the foolishness of investing in the desert.

An easy walking route with a feel of the wilderness about it.

Access by Bus

Bus Nº6 to the port in **Playa Blanca** and follow our western coastal promenade route to its end where Wp.8 of that route becomes Wp.1 of this route; add 2 hours to the total time.

Access by Car

From the petrol station roundabout at the end of the LZ2, go west on the dual carriageway to its seventh roundabout and then left, signed to **Villas Kamezi**. Straight over the next roundabout and then take the next left to arrive at the *faro* (lighthouse) and park, starting the walk at Wp.2.

Short Walk A
Faro de Pechiguera to the access path into **Faro Park** development, and then return by pavement through the new developments; 1 Walker, 1 hour.

Short Walk B
From the **Faro de Pechiguera**, follow the main route to the scruffy house at Wp.8 and marvel at the beautiful rock pools set in an exciting, and accessible, lava foreshore and return; 2 Walker, 1 hour 40 minutes.

Our start point is the western end of the coastal promenade (Wp.1 0M) where we step round the end of **Villas Kamezi** and cross open ground to come onto the remains of a tarmac road. At the end of the tarmac we go left on the dirt base of a new road, and then right on a smaller track to come to the twin light houses of **Faro de Pechiguera**, one small and squat and one tall and imperious, (Wp.2 11M). We work our way round the lighthouses to leave on a small path beside a low wall (Wp.3) which widens to a track which brings us up to a turning circle by the **Finistere** development (Wp.4 16M). Now we have the luxury of a promenade, but it does not last long and we are back on dirt track and trail until we climb over a boulder mound to come onto another turning circle (Wp.5 20M).

Now we are back on a better financed promenade, as we stroll between the foaming foreshore and the lifeless houses before coming to the access into **Faro Park** development (Wp.6 28M); for our Short Walk go right (E) at this junction.

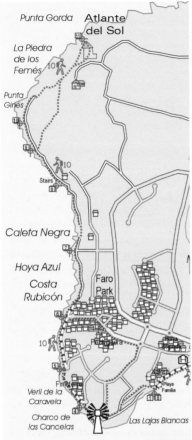

Punta Gorda   Atlante del Sol

La Piedra de los Femés

Punta Ginés

Stairs

Caleta Negra

Hoya Azul

Costa Rubicón

Faro Park

Finities

Veril de la Caravela

Charco de las Cancelas

Las Lajas Blancas

Punta Pechiguera

In another 188.6 metres, the promenade finishes along with the houses, and we have a scruffy little section before coming onto a track, taking a minor track ahead when the main track swings right, to cross a water runoff and come to a junction (Wp.7 40M) where a track goes right to the tarmac access road. Continuing ahead we pass an isolated house on its seaward side, the track ending for us to negotiate the end of the property's wall and a runoff before coming onto a trail paralleling the coast. Our trail widens to a track and views open up over the nothingness of the **Rubicón** desert as we head for another isolated house, recognisably scruffy even at this distance. As we close with the scruffy house, getting even scruffier as we close with it, the monstrous ugliness that is the **Atlante del Sol** comes into view. Coming up to the house (Wp.8 50M), we find a motley collection of caravans and vans seemingly attached to it, and a street name 'Cala Malva 1'; obviously owned by an optimist still awaiting the arrival of **Playa Blanca**'s outskirts.

As is the way of deserts, it is a surprise to find ugliness or nothingness, standing alongside something of great beauty - think of those **Papagayo** beaches backed by featureless, barren desert. It is the case here as, opposite the house, metal steps lead down the cliffs to a exciting lava foreshore containing beautiful rock pools.

Rock pools, fifty minutes into the walk.

From the house we continue along the track running above the cliffs, a branch going out onto a 'table' headland (Wp.9), the track becoming sandy as we pass a small lava peak (Wp.10), just after which is a bulldozed area where rocks have been heaped up and also a lava rock wall which serves no obvious purpose. It is almost as if we have passed into an illogical unreality as our track goes left in front of the wall while we go left on a trace of a track which soon peters out among the lava-topped cliffs. Ahead, our destination of **Atlante del Sol** seems close as we come inland to seek a route amongst the tracery of faint tracks and trails which dissect the rock-littered sandy desert.

We weave our way across the plain, passing a walled farm on our right to come on the unexpected sight of a swampy lagoon in front of the fire darkened shell of the hotel. Thinking 'Lord of the Rings' and 'Gates of Moria' we skirt the noisome waters to pass on the seaward side of the first

The swampy lagoon.

Amigos de Lourdes

wing and walk across the open ground to the far wing where we happen upon a small desert garden dedicated to the 'Amigos de Lourdes' (Wp.11 78M), another tiny touch of beauty juxtaposed against the massive ugliness of the **Atlante del Sol**.

Peña is strange Spanish word which doesn't really translate well into English. Perhaps the best we can offer is 'punishment' or 'inner pain', or 'torment', as when deciding between two unpleasant options. Standing by the financial and physical ruin that once was someone's expected boom town, we can appreciate the power of the desert and the ability of its nothingness to absorb even the best laid plans and investments.

You can continue from **Atlante del Sol** up the coastline, but add 12 kilometres to get to the **Salinas del Janubio**, most of this over rough ground, and then head for the **La Hoya** roundabout to wait for a bus. As most of this route is just much more of what we have experienced so far, we will leave it to the walking masochists.

For our return from **Atlante del Sol** we cut across the desert to Wp.9 and retrace our outward route back to the *faro*.

11. YAIZA'S VOLCANIC GARDENS

To commemorate the devastating volcanic eruptions of 1730-1736, in which the **Yaiza** region suffered the worst depredations, the local government built an elevated walkway and gardens running around the base of **Montaña Cinta**. This makes for easy strolling combined with views over the town to the lava sea and **Timanfaya**.

Unfortunately, they forgot to complete the centre section of the walkway, thus requiring us to do a little traditional path walking to join the two sections. They also forgot to tell anyone that these gardens exist, so although tour buses park near our start, you are likely to have the **Volcanic Gardens** and their views to yourself.

Access by Bus: The N°6 takes you into **Yaiza**.

Access by Car
Park off the old main road through **Yaiza** behind the church, where there is plenty of on-street parking and an official car park in front of the police station.

Short Walk
This <u>is</u> a short walk, but you can shorten it further by taking the stair access down to the old main road opposite **El Campo Bar/Restaurant**.

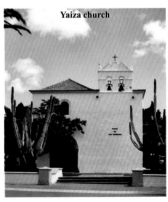

Yaiza church

We start out from the church (Wp.1 0M) to walk south past government administration buildings (note the 'Educación, Cultura y Festivos' office on the left, where you can pick up their 'Ruta de Cabellos' leaflet) to a multi-street junction with a confusion of traffic arrows painted on the roadway. On our front right is a lava wall containing planted gardens and a wide rock stairway, which we climb to come onto a broad red cinder track (Wp.2). The most energetic section of the route is already completed, as we turn right to stroll along the elevated walkway taking in the views over **Yaiza** town.

Our stroll curves around the hillside to the end of the first section of gardens (Wp.3), the second section of gardens facing us across a valley as we continue on a dirt track along the southern side of the valley. The fields on the valley floor are edged with earth mounds, and at the end of the second large field (Wp.4 10M) the track continues ahead while we go right onto a path which runs along the top of an earth mound (NW).

At the northern side of the field we swing right, dropping down to cross a gully

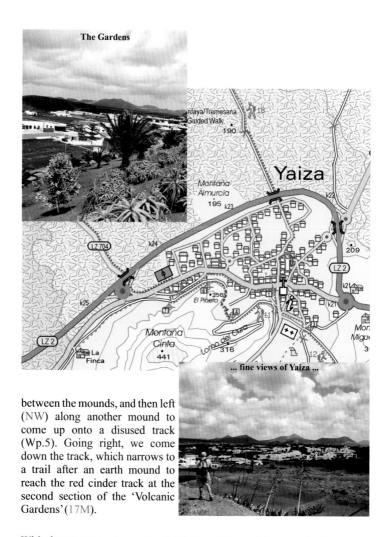

The Gardens

... fine views of Yaiza ...

between the mounds, and then left (NW) along another mound to come up onto a disused track (Wp.5). Going right, we come down the track, which narrows to a trail after an earth mound to reach the red cinder track at the second section of the 'Volcanic Gardens' (17M).

With the cross-country section behind us, it is back to easy strolling as we curve round the mountain to come above the **El Campo Bar/Rest**, where an access stairway drops down to the road (Wp.6); our Short Walk option. Both sections of the **Volcanic Gardens** have been well planted, the Aloe vera plants and Euphorbia varieties that line the track are particularly fine specimens, so it is a great disappointment when this planting runs out; the final section more a scene of crucifixion than planting, with young saplings staked out to die without water on the barren slopes.

At the end of this depressing section a dirt track continues round the mountain to **La Finca**, while we go right (Wp.7 25M) down a steep track that drops us down to the access road for the outlying houses of **Yaiza**. Once on the access track, we head right towards the old main road and **El Campo**, passing some scruffy houses before reaching the main road where we choose to take a refreshment stop in **El Campo Bar/Rest.** (Wp.8 30M). Our return is to simply walk along the pavement, up to our starting point at the church.

12. ATALAYA DE FEMÉS - LINEAR ROUTE

Femés remains our favourite village on Lanzarote. While we have the option of driving into the village and ascending the **Atalaya** by our unique circular route, we recognise that bus travellers and classicists like the traditional linear route. This is a long energetic ascent, as after the first kilometre every step is upwards until we reach the antennaed summit, from where we have a choice of returning by the same route to our start point or descending to **Femés**; our preference. Then to return to your start, we suggest our **Atalaya de Femés** - Circular route, until you meet up with your outward route.

While the **Atalaya de Femés** - Linear is one of the island's wilder routes, wayfinding is very straightforward. Virtually all the route is on clear tracks and paths, and if you do have any navigation questions, the answer is always 'uphill'.

*Distances are **Yaiza/Uga** - **Atalaya** 7 kilometres, **Atalaya** - **Femés** 2.7 kilometres, **Femés** - **Yaiza/Uga** 6.2 kilometres using the 'Circular' route.

Stroll
Volcanic Gardens (30 minutes, see text).

(There is no short version to this route.)

Access by Bus
Nº6 to **Yaiza** church on old main road, or entrance to **Uga**.

Access by Car
Park in the car park near the church in **Yaiza**.

 2CSK Route (see P.16)

Starting from **Yaiza**.
From outside the church (Wp.1 0M) we walk away from the old main road passing public buildings on each side; note the Cultura y Educación office on the left; to pass a large public square on our left and come to the junction at the top of the square (Wp.2). Ahead the road runs on to **La Degollada**, while on our front right are the **Volcanic Gardens**, built to commemorate the 250th anniversary of the **Timanfaya** eruption.

Stroll
Climbing the many steps, you will come onto a broad walkway which curves around the hillside giving views over **Yaiza** to the **Timanfaya**; surprisingly this gem is little visited by tourists. (See Walk 11, Yaiza's Volcanic Gardens)

From Wp.2, we follow the wide road left (ESE). When the tarmac changes to black *picon* grit (Wp.3), take a break to look up; our eyes are drawn to the massive *lomo* rising up to the **Atalaya** peak, it looks big and distant - both are true, but don't be daunted in your quest. We have easy striding across a plain before the track starts climbing, steadily at first but then steeper as a 'puff and grunt' ascent up to a junction by a giant tooth (Wp.4), once a complete windmill but seemingly more diminished each time we pass.

Starting from Uga

We start from opposite the village road junction with one of those quirky Spanish road junctions where you go right then attempt to cross the busy traffic to go right, instead of the logical turn left lane; see map. If you get off the bus at the church walk out past **Bar Gregorio** then left, right, left and up to carefully cross the main road.

From the southern side of the junction a dirt road leads up around a large house to a junction where the left hand track is 'Solo Camels'! Keeping left, we come onto a fertile plain after which our track runs along a valley floor as the ridges rise on each side of our route. Stark farm buildings, including camel farms, line the track until we come to a track off to the right heading toward a huge molar on the ridge above us. We turn up the track to climb up to a saddle and then up the line of the ridge to pass the remains of the old windmill and join our **Yaiza** route (Wp.4).

There is plenty of uphill ahead so you might want to take a first break on the windmill saddle, with views west across the **Valle de Fena** to the **Volcanic Gardens** and east down over the rather scruffy camel farms, before tackling the serious ascent ahead.

Combined Route

From the 'tooth', our black *picon* track runs straight up the spine in a steady ascent. When the black track goes down towards the **Femés** valley (Wp.5)we keep right on a rocky track, and then keep right at a second cairned track (Wp.6) which leads down into the valley, our return route. We keep right and uphill at these junctions with the **Atalaya** coming into view ahead. Surprisingly, we have a small downhill section before the ascent is rejoined, sections of **Femés** coming into sight along with views over the scattered houses and plots of **La Degollada**.

Our steady ascent brings us up onto a plateau on the wide ridge and for once the walking becomes an easy stroll as we saunter past rocky outcrops. These outcrops provide enough moisture and shelter for plant life to thrive, in contrast to the barren landscape we have been walking through. After skirting the outcrops, and with the peak's aerials ahead, our track dwindles to a path across a narrow section of the ridge and a small descent before we face a stiff 'puff and grunt' climb. The steep climb - stairs cut in the trail would be most useful - brings up onto a trackless plateau where cairns guide us front left over to the start of a faint track which takes us onto the **Atalaya**'s access road (Wp.7).

... the 'named' *caldera* ...

Once on the broad dirt road navigation, which has not been at all difficult to this point, becomes simplicity itself. We head up the broad track climbing up through a zigzag to look down into a 'named' *caldera*.

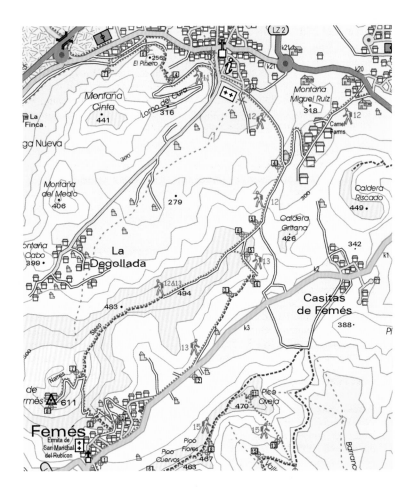

On the peak

It is then a straight uphill slog to the peak's trig point (Wp.8) beside the buildings and aerials. Going to the far end of the buildings we find a stepped path leading down to a cave house; just the place to take off your backpack and relax. The two small rooms and plastered walls appear to predate the transmitters, and a path leads on to a second smaller cave also shaped for habitation.

Descent to Femés

From the trig point, **Femés** village square looks both inviting and deceptively close. Our descent is so straightforward (we just head down the access track) that no description is necessary except to say, take care. The track is eroded in places and with a loose grit/dust surface in others making for a skittery descent with the possibility of being unceremoniously dumped on your bottom; we know! We pass our upward route (Wp.7 8M) and after a series of zig-zags we pass a track going steeply down to our right (Wp.9). After the chained vehicle barrier (30M) we come onto a village dirt road (Wp.10) to go right and pass the bottom of the track (Wp.11) we saw earlier. Reaching the village houses, we come onto tarmac/concrete streets where keeping straight ahead brings us into the village square and **Bar Femés** (Wp.12).

Return to **Yaiza/Uga**
Now, most walkers climb back up the access road to walk back down the ridge to their start point but unless you are a deliberate masochist who enjoys boring uphill climbs, then why not try something a little bit different with the start of our **Atalaya de Femes** - Circular route? It is certainly easier than the access road, and does mean that you are not repeating yourself.

We start out from **Bar Femés** (Wp.12 0M) by walking down the road (NE) away from the village. As the pavement ends (Wp.13 5M) we keep to the main road passing the lower section of the village on our left as easy strolling takes us down past a decorative palm garden before we come to a dirt track (Wp.14, 19M). We take the track to come above black *picon* fields and a hut (Wp.15 25M) just before the track runs out (28M) for us to come onto a narrow walking trail running behind the northern edge of the fields. A white painted cairn marks a small gully (Wp.16), cairns ahead of us marking our trail's route to climb up onto a spur of the main ridge. Across an affluent (Wp.17) and the trail is less distinct, as we ascend from the corner of the last field (Wp.18) to cross another affluent.

The furrowed landscape at waypoint 21

Across another two affluents (Wp.19&20) in this furrowed landscape and we are climbing the cairned path, the final cairn (Wp.21) appearing as a 'head & shoulders' from lower down the trail. A final climb brings us onto a broad *lomo* running south-east from the main ridge, with views over to **Puerto del Carmen**.

Now we start climbing in earnest. A faint track leads us up the *lomo* in a slogging ascent over the barren ground. onwards and upwards we come to a faint junction (Wp.22) where we keep right to connect with our outward route. From here it is all downhill to the windmill 'tooth', where it is down left for **Yaiza**, or onwards and down right for **Uga**.

13. ATALAYA DE FEMÉS CIRCUIT

Traditionally, the route up to the **Atalaya de Femés** is a linear one from either **Yaiza** or **Uga**, described in detail in our **Atalaya de Femés** - Linear Walk description. **Femés** is a beautiful village nestling in a fold at the top of the escarpment overlooking the **Rubicón** plain, easiest to reach by hire car. So here is a new circular route up the **Atalaya**, definitely both the simplest and most interesting way of taking in the peak.

Access by car; plenty of parking around **Femés** village square.

We start out from **Bar Femés** (Wp.1 0M 373 metres (closed Thursdays)) by walking down the road (NE) away from the village - yes, we <u>are</u> walking away from the mountain that we intend to climb. This seems more than a little crazy, but bear with us.

As the pavement ends (Wp.2 5M) we keep to the main road passing the lower section of the village on our left as we come to a bus shelter (Wp.3 12M). More easy strolling takes us down past a decorative palm garden before we come to a dirt track (Wp.4 19M). At last we leave the tarmac, taking to the track to come above black *picon* fields and a hut (Wp.5 25M) just before the track runs out (28M) for us to come onto a narrow walking trail running behind the northern edge of the fields. A white painted cairn marks a small gully (Wp.6), cairns ahead of us marking our trail's route to climb up onto a spur of the main ridge. Across an affluent (Wp.7), and now the trail is less distinct as we ascend from the corner of the last field (Wp.8) to cross another affluent. Across another two affluents (Wp.9 &10) in this furrowed landscape, and we are climbing the cairned path, the final cairn (Wp.11) resembling a 'head & shoulders' from lower down the trail. A final climb brings us onto a broad *lomo* running south-east from the main ridge, with views over to **Puerto del Carmen**.

Now we start climbing in earnest. A faint track leads us up the *lomo* in a slogging ascent over the barren ground. Onwards and upwards, we come to a faint junction (Wp.12). We keep straight ahead, but if returning to **Uga** or **Yaiza** swing right at the junction to connect with your outward route, the track dwindling to nothing as we cross the rock-littered open ground before coming onto the clear track of the traditional linear route running up the *lomo*.

Our steady ascent brings us up onto a plateau on the wide ridge and for once the walking becomes an easy stroll as we saunter past rocky outcrops. These outcrops provide enough moisture and shelter for plant life to thrive, in contrast to the barren landscape we have been walking through. After skirting the outcrops, and with the peak's aerials ahead, our track dwindles to a path across a narrow section of the ridge and a small descent before we face a stiff 'puff and grunt' climb. The steep climb - stairs cut in the trail would be most useful - brings us up onto a trackless plateau where cairns guide us front left over to the start of a faint track which takes us onto the **Atalaya**'s access road (Wp.13).

Once on the broad dirt road navigation, which has not been at all difficult to this point, becomes simplicity itself. We head up the broad track climbing up through a zigzag to look down into a 'named' *caldera* and then straight uphill slog to the peak's trig point (Wp.14) beside the buildings and aerials. Going to the far end of the buildings we find a stepped path leading down to a cave house; just the place to take off your backpack and relax. The two small rooms and plastered walls appear to predate the transmitters, and a path leads on to a second smaller cave also shaped for habitation.

Descent to **Femés**

From the trig point, **Femés** village square looks both inviting and deceptively close. Our descent is so straightforward (we just head down the access track) that no description is necessary except to say, take care. The track is eroded in places and with a loose grit/dust surface in others making for a skittery descent with the possibility of being unceremoniously dumped on your bottom; we know!

Descent to Femés

We pass our upward route (Wp.13 8M) and after a series of zig-zags we pass a track going steeply down to our right (Wp.15). After the chained vehicle barrier (30M) we come onto a village dirt road (Wp.16) to go right and pass the bottom of the track (Wp.17) we saw earlier. Reaching the village houses, we come onto tarmac/concrete streets where keeping straight ahead brings us into the village square and **Bar Femés** (Wp.1).

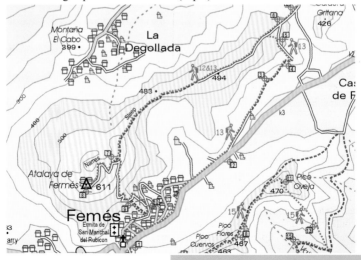

14. THE HIDDEN BARRANCOS

Safe from the depredations of tourism is a region of barren grandeur comprising the **Higuera** and **Casita** *barrancos*. Ten years ago when we discovered this route it was little known, though now it has become relatively popular with energetic walkers. The only development since we first walked the route consists of a basic refuge near its half way point. It might be called a refuge but it offers negligible shade, so set out well protected and with plenty of water for this adventure in the wilderness. Clear paths make for easy route finding, with the exception of finding our outward path by the goat farm.

Access	**Short Walk**
By car, park in **Femés**.	Follow the route in reverse to ascend **Pico Aceituna** and return the same way. 1.5 hours, 4 kilometres, 200 metres ascents/descents.

We start in the village of **Femés** outside the bar of the same name. Across the 'main' road we start out on a tarmac road (Wp.1 0M 376 metres) heading south (S) towards a ridge topped with an ugly farm. The tarmac soon gives way to dirt as we start a slogging ascent up towards the farm, passing two paths on our right (Wps. 2&3) before struggling up to the end of the track beside the goat farm on the ridge (Wp.4 7M) to look down into the **Barranco de la Higuera**. Here the ground is churned up by the goats which can confuse the confuseable as to where the path is. Keeping the main farm and corral on our left, we step to the edge of the ridge.

The start of the descent

Away on our right is our return path, clearly outlined against the rock, while below us our dusty narrow path drops down into the *barranco*. It is a skittery descent on the loose, goat-churned surface, dropping past multi-hued rocks to turn below **Pico Aceituna** (and the return path) to start a zigzag descent down to a cobbled section (18M).

Now we are on an undulating easy section of path which heads towards an electricity pylon, **Puerto Calero** coming into view in the distance. We wind steadily downhill, passing nicotiana plants struggling to survive in this barren landscape.

Passing a path to our left (Wp.5 27M) (our 1995 route, and an option to finish in **Playa Quemada**) we start turning into and out of the affluents which feed the main *barranco* before we come under the pylon to step onto an old jeep track (30M). A path connects sections of the old track as we follow the line of the pylons; ahead we can see our trail's extension as we pass a path coming up

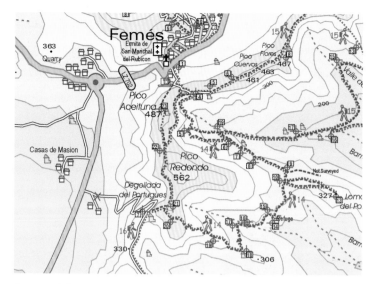

from our left (Wp.6, our 1995 route) before coming down to a second pylon. From the pylon, we ignore traces heading into the *barranco* as we start heading up the main path which climbs up past a crumbling corral (Wp.7) and crossing an affluent (Wp.8) before a slogging ascent brings us up past great swathes of asphodels to meet the ridge's crest at a broad saddle.

On reaching the saddle we find a wide stone littered plain, on our left another trace/path down to **Playa Quemada** (Wp.9) while our route continues ahead as a swept path through the rock litter. An easy stroll takes us over to a junction (Wp.10 55M) where a jeep track and a path head left (E) to the small peak of **Morro de la Loma del Pozo**.

Having come this far it would be foolish to ignore the extension to the *morro* (literally, the snout or nose) so we head out on the narrow path, an easy stroll until we close with the peak where the gradient increases (Wp.11) by the first outcrop. The jeep track comes up to join us (Wp.12) - not that you would want to drive anything on this track - for a steep ascent up to a pair of large cairns which mark the summit (Wp.13 66M). We return to the junction (Wp.10 80M) on the jeep track.

Back on the main route, we head SW on the path, the refuge coming into sight like a mirage in this barren expanse. Our path heads down through an affluent to bring us to the refuge (Wp.14 86M), perched on the edge of the **Barranco de la Casita**.

Relaxing at the refuge

We give thanks to the authorities who have constructed a refuge in the middle of nowhere, and honour the construction with our presence for a break; if only they had put a proper roof on it to provide some meaningful shade. Relaxing at the refuge, we can appreciate the subtle variations of the rock hues in this arid environment, as well as contemplating the task ahead of us as we sit under the looming presence of **Pico Redondo**.

From the refuge (0M) we follow the path as it winds down into a gully (Wp.15), after which our path unwinds along the side of the big *barranco*, crossing a couple of affluents before coming into the *barranco* proper to run down to cross the line of the watercourse (Wp.16). Standing on the floor of the *barranco* we appreciate that the next stage is of necessity energetic. All around us the land rises up to high ridges and to **Pico Redondo**, none of it vertical but all of it muscle-sapping steep. Looking up the *barranco* we can see our next objective, the high saddle to left of **Pico Redondo**, and very high up it appears from this viewpoint.

Our broad path angles up the southern slope before swinging left (Wp.17) for a long traverse up onto the ridge which separates us from **Barranco de los Dises**, a 'puff and grunt' ascent up through zigzags bringing us onto the ridge by an old corral (Wp.18 17M 295 metres) to look longingly back to the refuge. Now our path heads straight up the ridge, getting rougher as we come up to pass a rocky peak thick with asphodels (Wp.19 343 metres). Ahead, our path zigzags up a steeper section of the *lomo*, yet another 'puff and grunt' ascent, taking breaks at each turn.

... bemused goats ...

This relentless slog up the *lomo* is brightened by the flocks of goats of all shades and sizes that we always find on this ridge. The goats are not quite pettable but give a bemused look at us strange bipeds who make such hard work of the rocky ground that they simply skip over. Eventually our ascent brings us up onto the saddle between **Pico Redondo** and **Hacha Grande** (Wp.20 48M 449 metres).

From the saddle, a narrow path curves right around the peak's western slopes to bring us above a goat farm set on a saddle fifty metres below us. We come down to a path junction (Wp.21 52M) where the **Femés-Papagayo** alternative route goes down to the farm and dirt road. Keeping right, our narrow path, and a black water pipe, curve round a steep bowl (possibly vertiginous for some) past bands of soft hued rock before a short ascent takes us over a spur into a smaller bowl. **Pico Aceituna** is ahead as we come up past deep purple rock to emerge onto the saddle between **Redondo** and **Aceituna**. (Wp.22 72M).

Here we take a diversion off the main route to climb **Pico Aceituna**. A faint path leads up the lower slopes but soon disappears amongst the rocks. We simply keep climbing straight up, picking our steps over the rocks to come onto the summit (Wp.23) beside a large stone corral which has been built in this least likely location. From the northern end of the peak we look down on **Femés**, while the views over the **Rubicón** plain to **Playa Blanca** and Fuerteventura are a fitting reward for this small ascent.

It is possible to scramble down the northern face of the peak - possible, but not recommended, and so we retrace our upward route back to the saddle (Wp.22). We leave the saddle on a narrow path dropping down into the **Barranco de la Higuera**, our route curving round beneath **Aceituna** before climbing up to the goat farm ridge by a second building. We take a path down the slope in front of the building to join the dirt road for a relaxed stroll down to the village centre, where a choice of refreshment opportunities should not be overlooked; **Bar Femés** is closest and least touristy.

15. FEMÉS RIDGE

Femés is a favourite with us, especially if **Bar Femés** is open. Back in '95, our 'Hidden Barrancos' route pioneered walking in the **Higuera** and **Casita** *barrancos*, our route now appearing in Landscapes and Cicerone books. For Walk! Lanzarote, we sought out a very special route as our new 'classic' of the region, the 'Femés Ridge', is that route.

The **Femés Ridge** is one of the few Lanzarote routes where you get close to a high mountain feeling, yet we reach the mountain peak in a relatively relaxed manner on a little-known path, plus some open ground climbing. We have magnificent views from **Pico Oveja** (Sheep Peak) over the southern peaks, before descending into the valleys. You cannot get that high - and that low - on a circular route, without the inevitable uphill finish; a long slog up through the old *Majo* settlement in the **Barranco de la Higuera**. Quite simply, a modern classic route for experienced walkers.

4 | 3 H | 8 km | 550m / 550m | ⟳ | ⚠ | 0

Access by Car
Park in the centre of **Femés** near the church square.

> **Short Walk**
> To **Pico Oveja** and return
> (3 Walker, 1¾ hours).

From **Bar Femés** (Wp.1 0M) we cross the main road to head up the dirt track towards the ugly goat farm sat on the ridge. A slogging ascent, up between the water tanks (Wp.2) and a trail off to our right (Wp.3), brings us up to the farm's modern door entrance (Wp.4 7M), where we continue along the track (E) to head over a crest to a second farm (Wp.5 12M) with noisy chained dogs.

The track ends as we continue on the northern side of the ridge following a trail - really a mere trace of a goat trail - to maintain height as we head towards the first of the peaks. When one trace finishes we simply step onto another, a path gradually emerging as we come below the first peak (Wp.6), a rocky scramble if you want to take in the views.

Timanfaya Fire Mountains ahead

Black *picon* fields dot the **Femés Valley** below us, while ahead in the distance are the **Timanfaya Fire Mountains** (**Montañas del Fuego**), but no views south until the rocky ridge runs down to a 'rock free' crest where we step up from the path to marvel at the southern landscapes (Wp.7/8). Back on the path, we maintain height until our path starts running downhill to a saddle, the surface becoming rock-littered and slowing our progress, before disappearing entirely in a maze of goat traces. From the saddle, we climb up to a boulder-mounted cairn on the ridge (Wp.8 28M) for more breathtaking views into the valleys.

From the cairn, we continue along the ridge saddle past a pair of *zoco* style small corrals, a faint path emerging as the ridge rises again on our right to **Pico Oveja**. Maintaining height, we see ahead that our trail runs down, becoming more defined as it descends to meet a trail from **Casitas de Femes** on a broad saddle.

Now it is decision time, as we go uphill over open ground and goat traces, aiming for an old terrace (Wp.9); there a few of these small boulder supported terraces, but simply head for the highest one. Continuing diagonally uphill towards the line of the ridge, we cross another terrace before coming up to a low stone wall (Wp.10) which runs up the ridge. Now we follow the wall until it gives out, from where a 'puff and grunt' ascent brings us up to **Pico Oveja** (Wp.11 55M).

Wonderful views from Pico Oveja

Stepping around the peak itself, we move from a comparatively gentle landscape to an orogenical one. After that climb it would be a waste to immediately strike off down into the valleys, and even though there is plenty of proof that the peak is popular with goats, we find some suitable ledges at a comfortable height on the southern side, on which to be seated while taking in the views. From our vantage point on the peak we can see the trail coming over the saddle from **Casitas de Femés**, our first objective on the descent. This is pathless country with a picky descent, steep in places before we reach the path, so if in doubt, return by our outward route to **Femés**.

We strike off from the peak (0M) along the line of the ridge (SE) carefully picking our way down to where the ridge broadens into a rock-littered *lomo*. Keeping direction (SW), we stroll down the *lomo*, surrounded by superb views, to its 'nose' (Wp.12). The steep 'nose' calls for care as we pick our way down over loose rock and boulders. Taking a break on this picky descent we can see the trail from **Casitas** coming over a saddle, still a long way ahead and down from our position.

At the base of the 'nose' we look back at the line of our descent - it looks almost sheer from below (!), before resuming a strolling descent of the rock-littered *lomo* to pass the remains of a corral (Wp.13) and finally come down to the trail (Wp.14 36M), positively a 'walking motorway' in these pathless expanses. From here you could turn left for **Casitas** and return to **Femés** on the road, an easier but less spectacular route than what we have ahead.

Once on the path, we follow it right, our route feeling comfortably luxurious

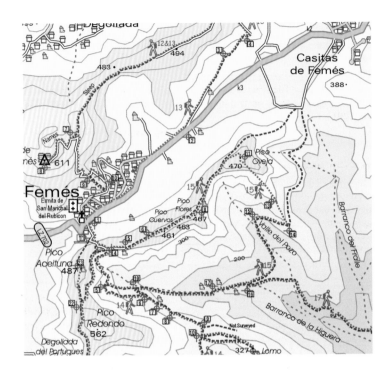

after the *lomo*, to start dropping (NW) into the **Valle del Pozo**. After heading up the valley, gradually descending, we come down to cross a water runoff by an old stone wall (Wp.15 41M). Across the runoff, our trail swings left (S/SE) down towards the main valley and a line of small electricity pylons. Our faint path crosses another runoff and follows old stone walls, this section giving a wonderful sense of spaciousness as we stroll down to cross more runoffs before swinging right (S/SW) into the main valley where we come alongside a jeep track, which our path joins by an electricity pylon (Wp.16 52M).

We've been descending continuously for nearly an hour, and now we face the consequences in the form of a long uphill slog along the **Barranco de la Higuera**. Setting off from the pylon we follow the jeep track beside the broad water runoff. As we climb this relentless ascent, we start to pass old corrals and stone walls before crossing the runoff (Wp.17) which now becomes a small gorge on our right. Technically, the jeep track should be an easy section of our route, but it doesn't feel like it as we labour up past pylons, corrals and stone walls before crossing an affluent (Wp.18) which brings the hideous goat farms into view high up on the ridge ahead; and before you ask the answer is, 'Yes, we do have to climb up there.'.

The remains of corrals and buildings litter the valley floor, some thought to be remains of *Majo* settlements (the eastern Canary Islands' equivalent of the western islands' *Guanches*), predating the Spanish invasion. A second division of this agricultural settlement was based around the *barranco* mouth at **Playa del Pozo**. There have been some archaeological investigations made of these ruins, and their *Majo* heritage seems well proven.

We keep slogging up the rough jeep track, passing a trail off to our left (our original route in 'The Hidden Barrancos') (Wp.19) and crossing an affluent where the track swings up to our left and we continue ahead on a clear trail (Wp.20).

The path junction at 94 minutes

This trail climbs steeply up to join our 'Hidden Barrancos' route at a path junction (Wp.21 94M), which provides us with a good place to take a break before tackling the final ascent up to the farms.

From the junction, our narrow trail climbs steeply (N), though this style of ascent is more pleasing than the jeep track, and is enlivened by the wonderful geological examples that we pass before finally emerging from the head of the *barranco* beside the farm (Wp.4 110M). After that long and energetic ascent, we stumble back down the dirt track and across the road to fall into **Bar Femés** (Wp.1 115M) for some well earned refreshment, where we can relive the wonders of this modern classic that we've just completed.

The long route out of **Playa Blanca** via **Papagayo** beach and up the dirt track to the **Degollada del Portugués**, followed by path and track into **Femés**, is one of Lanzarote's classic long distance routes. Like many of the island's long linear routes, accessibility is a problem. After an initial climb out of **Femés** we skirt around **Pico Aceituna** on our 'Hidden Barrancos' route (Walk 14) in reverse, before dropping down to the **Degollada del Portugués**. From this pass, we stroll down a dirt track to emerge from the mountains onto the far south of the **Rubicón** desert plain. Our official route then wanders along the coast, with the opportunity of testing the famous beaches of this region, before heading into **Playa Blanca** on the return route of Walk 9 and Walk 7 to reach the 'old town'.

Both Noel Rochford (Landscapes) and Paddy Dillon (Cicerone) describe this route as an energetic uphill from **Playa Blanca**. Why they should choose to travel this route by the most difficult approach is a mystery to us.

Access from **Playa Blanca**: taxi to **Femés**.

Access by Bus: Nº6 bus to **Playa Blanca** and then taxi to **Femés**, unless you manage to catch the Nº5 8.00 bus from **Arrecife** which does stop at **Femés**.

Access by Car: drive to **Femés**, and park by the village square and taxi back from **Playa Blanca**.

2CSK Route (see P.16) but make sure you start from **Femés** end of the route. Park the lower car as for Walk 9 **Papagayo**, and reduce distance to 19 kilometres.

We start out from **Bar Femés** (Wp.1 0M); if you walking our routes in order, you will be a well known regular in this little bar by now. Following Walks 14 & 15 up onto the ridge (Wps.2 & 3), we then take Walk 14 in reverse (Wp.4 11M) to come onto the pass between **Pico Aceituna** and **Pico Redondo** (Wp.5 24M). The path below **Pico Redondo** is a little trickier, and might cause vertigo sufferers a little trouble, before reaching the path junction (Wp.6) above the goat farm, where we follow the black water pipe down past the farm and onto the **Degollada del Portugués** (Wp.7 43M).

A track, barred to vehicle access, climbs up from the **Rubicón** desert plain through a series of zigzags before crossing the *degollada* to run down the **Barranco de los Dises**. We stroll down the track, passing another *degollada* viewpoint at the head of the *barranco* before coming under the bulk of **Hacha Grande** to snake in and out of sharp clefts in the mountain.

This is an easy strolling route downhill, but a rather depressing slogging ascent if you were to follow Rochford or Dillon's directions. Little climbs

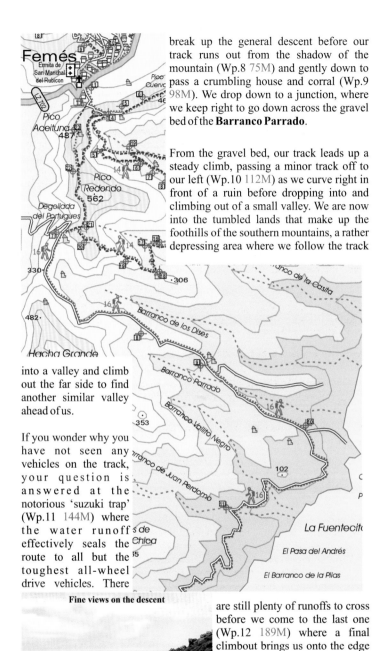

break up the general descent before our track runs out from the shadow of the mountain (Wp.8 75M) and gently down to pass a crumbling house and corral (Wp.9 98M). We drop down to a junction, where we keep right to go down across the gravel bed of the **Barranco Parrado**.

From the gravel bed, our track leads up a steady climb, passing a minor track off to our left (Wp.10 112M) as we curve right in front of a ruin before dropping into and climbing out of a small valley. We are now into the tumbled lands that make up the foothills of the southern mountains, a rather depressing area where we follow the track into a valley and climb out the far side to find another similar valley ahead of us.

If you wonder why you have not seen any vehicles on the track, your question is answered at the notorious 'suzuki trap' (Wp.11 144M) where the water runoff effectively seals the route to all but the toughest all-wheel drive vehicles. There

Fine views on the descent

are still plenty of runoffs to cross before we come to the last one (Wp.12 189M) where a final climbout brings us onto the edge of the **Rubicón** desert plain at a track junction (Wp.13 197M).

From the foot of the mountains we look out over the hazy plain to the headland bar above **Papagayo** beach and the white scars that are the eastern outskirts of **Playa Blanca**, and we have a problem. Until now, wayfinding has simply meant keeping to the main track, but now we have a plethora of tracks and trails to choose from but with few identifiable landmarks to guide us.

If you want the quickest way to the bar, then follow a track WSW and then forking S to come onto the main track serving the **Papagayo** parking area. Our scenic route is to go SE on a track and then follow the coastal paths - plenty to chose from, to either drop into beaches such as **El Pasito** (a strange glitch has caused to lose our GPS track at this point; possibly distracted by naturists, I forgot to power up after taking a break on the beach), or pass above the bays where possible. Our scenic route is a bit longer in distance and time for us to arrive at the **Papagayo** bars (Wp.14 253M).

Our final objective, Playa Blanca, is in sight

From **Papagayo** we follow Walk 9 back to the road system below the **Papagayo Arena Hotel** (1.5 km 45M). On the roads follow the blue 'Papagayo Beach' signs in reverse down to a small roundabout, and then on walkways down to the pebble beach of **Playa del Afe**; you could reach this point by staying to seaward of the hotel, and descending on paths directly onto the beach.

From the end of the beach the coastal promenade (Walk 7) starts to guide you back into the centre of **Playa Blanca** at the 'old town' (4 kilometres +60M). By the time you have finished six hours of continuous hiking, you will certainly have earned some reward for your efforts, and you'll be glad you chose the 'downhill' option!

17. FEMÉS TO PLAYA QUEMADA - THE MISSING LINK

Having pioneered the 'Hidden Barrancos' (Walk 14) route over ten years ago, we are pleased to add the exciting circular route 'Femés Ridge' (Walk 15), and this very pleasant linear route from **Femés** to **Playa Quemada** to our repertoire. After the ascent up to the 'goat farm' ridge, it's all downhill along the **Barranco de la Higuera** to **Playa del Pozo** and a final section on the tracks and trails of our 'Playa del Pozo' (Walk 22) route to finish in **Playa Quemada**. There's a slight risk of vertigo in the early stages of the route (see Walk 14 'Hidden Barrancos').

Note that on the Tour & Trail Map section we do not show the waypoints for this walk, as another part set of numbers would simply confuse in what is becoming a very busy region of the island for walking routes.

The opening up of this easy linear route presents a myriad of opportunities to combine sections of our 14, 15 and 17 routes with other paths in the region to produce a wide variety of 'pick & mix' walking combinations.

Access by Bus: bus N°6 to **Yaiza** and taxi to **Femés** (there is a limited bus service to **Femés**, but you'd have to catch the 08.00 N°5 from **Arrecife** to make this route feasible by bus.)

Access by Car: park either by the square in **Femés** or in **Playa Quemada** near where the road swings right by the first restaurant. In either case you will have to re-walk the route to get back to your car; so it's probably best to start in **Playa Quemada** - then you get an easy return after lunch.

It is our usual start after coffee at **Bar Femés** (Wp.1 0M), to climb up the track to the ugly goat farm (Wps.2&3) from where we take the 'Hidden Barrancos' trail (Wp.4 9M) down into the head of the **Barranco de la Higuera**. Dropping swiftly down below **Pico Aceituna**, we come to the path junction (Wp.5 16M) to go left down the *barranco* on our 'Femés Ridge' route in reverse; a much easier option than the ascent on Walk 15. An easy strolling descent takes us down (Wps.6&7) past the remains of the Guanche settlements to the pylon path junction (Wp.8 39M) where our 'Femés Ridge' route comes in from the **Valle del Pozo**.

Keeping to the jeep track, we move away from the line of the water runoff in the *barranco* (E) until we meet the run off from **Valle del Pozo** to swing right (SSW) towards **Playa del Pozo**. We come back to the **Barranco de la Higuera** runoff (Wp.9 50M) to head down the broad valley, crossing the mouth of the **Barranco del Fraile** (Wp.10 63M) to come to the track climbing up the eastern wall (Wp.11).

Approaching Playa Quemada

Now we are on our 'Playa del Pozo' route leaving the track (Wp.12) and following the paths across the headlands and *barrancos* (Wps.13 & 14) to come to the outskirts of the **Playa Quemada** settlement (Wp.15 95M). Rather than follow the roads, we take the coastal path across to the sea front houses and restaurant (Wps.16, 17&18 105M).

The most difficult thing about this walk is getting a place on the walk itself. This is the official guided walk in the **Timanfaya** and you need to book by phoning the Visitors' Centre on 928-840839, or calling in person; the centre is on the LZ67 road south of **Tinajo** and **Mancha Blanca**. Numbers are limited to two mini buses, each carrying seven walkers. Given the increasing popularity of this guided walk, it is getting even more difficult to secure one of the fourteen places available so we recommend phoning (00-34-928-840839 when dialling from outside Spain), well before you leave for Lanzarote. You will need to reconfirm your place on the walk the day before by phone or visit.

Access by Car: on the LZ67 road from **Yaiza** to **Mancha Blanca**. Drive past the entrance to **Timanfaya National Park**, and the Visitors' Centre is the next major building on your left, 3.5 kilometres further along the road. Make sure you arrive before the 10.00 start.

2CSK Route (see P.16)

Assuming you have managed the rather difficult task of securing a place, then at 10.00 it is all aboard the two buses, followed by a long drive via **Yaiza**.

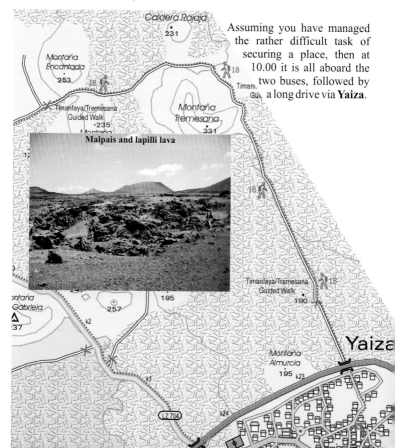

Malpais and lapilli lava

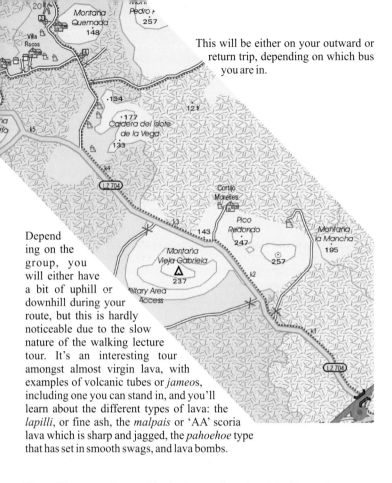

This will be either on your outward or return trip, depending on which bus you are in.

Depending on the group, you will either have a bit of uphill or downhill during your route, but this is hardly noticeable due to the slow nature of the walking lecture tour. It's an interesting tour amongst almost virgin lava, with examples of volcanic tubes or *jameos*, including one you can stand in, and you'll learn about the different types of lava: the *lapilli*, or fine ash, the *malpais* or 'AA' scoria lava which is sharp and jagged, the *pahoehoe* type that has set in smooth swags, and lava bombs.

The guides are well versed in the facts and myths of the **Timanfaya** as we stroll through the unique landscape on this strolling lecture tour. They park the buses at each end of the manicured track and swap keys when they meet - wonder where they got that idea from? If they think you are capable, (basically, if all of you look like you can walk and there are no 'couch potatoes' in the group) they will do the full 'there and back' walk of six kilometres in only a little more than the one way time. For everyone interested in the historical and volcanic background of the **Timanfaya**, this is a 'Must Do' tour, though you will have to sift the fact from myth; for example, if …"a footstep takes three years to disappear …." then why is there no sign of the workers' footmarks who created this manicured track?

At the risk of exposing yourself to Lanzarote's 'lava police', you could walk the route yourself without guides. Just <u>saying</u> this is possibly a treasonable offence on Lanzarote, but the track is open to public access. At each end a padlocked chain bars vehicle access, for which the guides and farmers have keys, but it is open for walkers. If you cannot get a place on the official walk, or would be unhappy at the very pedestrian pace, simply park at one end of the access track and walk in and back; alternatively, be a two car group and park a car at each end and swap keys when you meet amongst the lava.

19. MONTAÑA CUERVO - A GEM IN LANZAROTE'S CROWN

Once in a while we discover an absolute gem of a walking route, something not in any other guide book, and which even the authorities have missed. **Montaña Cuervo** is just such a gem, so much so that if you miss this little route you will miss much of what Lanzarote has to offer. Vulcanologists will marvel at the condition of the exploded volcanic cone, while the rest of us simply stare in awe at the truly spectacular *caldera*.

Don't try to compare this natural wonder with the sanitised **Timanfaya** bus ride or closely guided walks - nothing compares to **Montaña Cuervo**.

Judging by the access track and the car park near the cone, the authorities might be planning to make this another 'loads-a-money' attraction, so best to see this natural wonder now while it is as free as the Lanzarote wind.

Access by car: On the LZ56 park on the roadside just north of the **Tías/Tinajo** municipal boundary markers, or pull into the car parking area on the east of the road a few metres further north.

Short Walk

This walk is already short, but if you are only interested in the truly spectacular, then go into the *caldera* and return, remembering the path over the lava field on your return.

Extended Walk

Dirt tracks branch off our circular route enabling you to explore more of the 'lava sea' of this region. Where our track meets the cone at Wp.2, a *picon* path climbs to the lip of the crater: a gritty ascent and slidey descent which we do not recommend.

We leave the LZ56 on a well-stabilised track (Wp.1 0M), stepping over or round the chain barring vehicle access to head west towards the small mountain. **Montaña Cuervo** is not a big mountain, but rising up out of the lava sea, its sharp image contrasts with the fuzzy lava, lending it a mystical presence even from this distance.

The mystical Montaña Cuervo

An easy stroll along the cinder track takes us past a faint track, off to our right, to swing left and then right to come to the base of the cone (Wp.2 6M) where another track goes off to the right (N). We shun the steep *picon* path climbing to the lip of the crater and follow our track around the cone (NNW), a lava

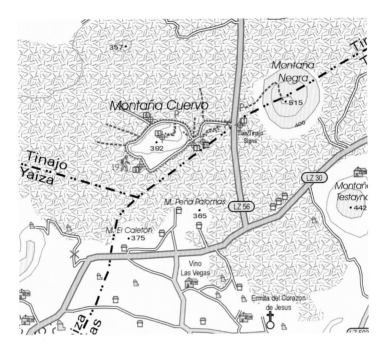

'wave' cutting out the views as we pass another steep *picon* path ascending the crater shortly before coming to a surprise (Wp.3 10M); not the large car parking area on the right, but the huge gash in the side of the volcanic cone which gives access to its interior.

To descend the path beneath huge volcanic boulders into the *caldera* is to enter another world. From the road, you would never guess that this stunning interior landscape of a volcano was awaiting you.

Inside the crater ... a surreal experience

From our viewpoint on the floor of the crater (Wp.4), the geology is simply awesome, while at the western end of the crater (110 metres away at Wp.5) wild pink geraniums colonise the floor and slopes, adding to the unreality of this surreal experience.

People spend hours in this crater where time has little meaning, so when you choose to depart we will restart our timing at the crater entrance (Wp.3 0M) as we head west around the cone on a broad *picon* trail running between the mountain and the lava 'wave' on our right. The wave is broken by a track (Wp.6) which heads towards **Timanfaya**, the break giving us a chance to look out over this great 'lava sea'.

As we circle the extended cone, we pass another track going out into lava fields (Wp.7 8M) and admire more colonies of wild geraniums blooming in the most unforgiving landscape you could imagine, particularly numerous in one floriferous area seemingly at odds with the surroundings, which also sustains Vinagrera (Rumex lunaria), Lanzarote Firebush or Aulaga (Launaea arborescens), and Nicotiana glauca.

Our track runs gently downhill past a track heading out into the lava (Wp.8) and curves around the mountain (SSE), then passing a series of lava ledges (Wp.9) on our right, clearly indicating the thin, harder surfaced crusts above a softer core that you'll be warned not to step on if you take the **Timanfaya** guided walk. We crunch along on the *picon* trail curving (WNW) towards the main bulk of the mountain rising above cinder dunes, the dunes and cinder slopes being replaced by bedrock (Wp.10) shortly before we come back to our outward route (21M) beside the path which climbs to the crater rim.

Strolling back towards the LZ56, we notice a trail marked by an arrow of stones (Wp.11 24M), a junction we missed on our way outward. We turn off the track onto the path which then wanders through the broken crust of the lava field giving a real, up close and personal view of lava ledges and collapsed crust, before coming back to our outward track 139.4 metres (approximately, thanks to the accuracy of our GPS survey system) from the start of the track beside the main road. Arriving back at our car, we can only marvel at this 'gem' of an easy walking route, almost literally in the middle of nowhere.

20. A PATH BETWEEN TWO SEAS - THE TIMANFAYA COASTAL PATH

Our third **Timanfaya** route has a surreal nature all of its own for most of the route, as we walk along a coastal path between the Atlantic Ocean on our right and the 'Lava Sea' on our left. It is long and linear so best suited to our 2CSK approach (see P.16).

We start at the achingly lovely **Playa Madera**, and twelve kilometres later emerge from the lava sea below a beautiful villa set on a hill in the middle of nowhere. Good walking footwear is essential for this rocky lava trail if you are to avoid bruising the soles of your feet. Note that access has to be by car.

Access by Car:

From **Tinajo** take the minor road towards **Tenesar** coastal settlement. When the road turns sharp right, continue straight ahead on a wide, but corrugated, dirt road. Ignore all side turnings, and as the surface changes to *picon* look for somewhere to park; note this is six kilometres of bumpy dirt road from when you leave the luxurious tarmac. On no account try to drive down to the beach area at **Playa Madera**.

> **Short Walk**
> Take the path from either end and walk as far as you like as an out and back route.

From **Yaiza** take the LZ704 road to **El Golfo**. The easiest way to identify the dirt road that you need, is to drive to the junction before **El Golfo**, signed left to **La Hoya**, turn around and the dirt road is the first one on the left as you head back towards **Yaiza**. Turn onto the dirt road and pass two chained tracks right (the first is for the **Timanfaya** guided walk) and one left and then start looking for a parking place off the track before reaching the villa set on the slopes of **Montaña Quemada**.

Playa Madera

From your parking place, walk down the track onto **Playa Madera** (Wp.1 0M), a wonderfully isolated black beach with the Atlantic waves crashing onto the edge of the 'Lava Sea', and climb up the path onto the lava sea.

This is a wonderful setting, with the ocean crashing against the lava and small lava points on our right, while on our left the 'lava sea' rolls away to the distant 'fire mountains' of **Timanfaya**. Amongst the lava sea are points of higher

ground around which the slow moving lava flowed, known locally as *islotes:* these green islands harbour local flora which stand out in sharp contrast against the barren lava.

That is about as poetic as it gets, because while the setting is dramatic, with the ocean battling the lava sea, it is very much all the same. Here, they have lava in abundance forming a massive jagged plain, and the only way across this impenetrable expanse is the coastal path. So it is onward, one step after another along the rocky path, stopping occasionally to take in the views, which all seem remarkably like the views you stopped for earlier. It is a strange combination of beauty and monotony. We can walk for what seems like ages and then look around, and we have the rather disconcerting feeling that we haven't moved since the last stop, the immediate landscape being ocean and jagged lava sea. This weird impression of not making any progress can be somewhat disturbing, but keep going.

We have 9.5 kilometres of this beautiful but monotonous landscape, before **Montaña Halcones** rises out of the jagged sea on our left, indicating that we will soon be leaving the sea. Our path finally turns away from the ocean and winds along (SSE) to meet a dirt track. Now the landscape starts to change as the lava sea gives way to fig trees in *zocos* and occasional cultivated plots as our route heads towards **Montaña Quemada** (SE), climbing gently to bring us up to a vehicle barrier (Wp.2 176M). Even the isolated farming plots seem like the height of civilisation after all that jagged lava, as we walk up to pass beneath a luxury villa (Wp.3 182M) set on the slopes of **Montaña Quemada** above our track. Having climbed up the slope of the mountain, the track now runs down to a junction of tracks (Wp.4 188M) marked by concrete gate posts with a small commemorative shrine set in them.

Where you go from the junction depends on where you choose to finish. 2CSK walkers (see P.16) should find the second car somewhere along the onward track (SE). If you plan to finish in **Yaiza**, then take this onward track to meet the LZ704 tarmac road, and turn left for 4.5 kilometres of road walking to the big roundabout, now taking the old main road signed for **Yaiza**, for another kilometre to find the first refreshments opposite the football pitch and showground on the town's outskirts.

If you are seeking the closest civilisation or refreshment, go right at the junction. The track undulates along past farmsteads (W) before swinging left (S) to meet the LZ704. Turn right and in under a kilometre you are in **El Golfo** with a choice of tourist style *tipicos* to choose from; you should also find a taxi or two here, or ask in a bar.

nino

aldro

plida

Parque Na

rejos

△ Montaña
Halcones
105

Islote de Halcones

La Mesa

Playa del Paso

Montaña de
Pedro Perico
257

20

Montaña
Quemada
148

a del Jurado

Villa
Rocos

El Golfo

·134

·177
Caldera del Islote
de la Vega
·133

Montaña
del Golfo
155

k5

Charco de los Clicos

The unique agricultural landscape of **La Geria** is one of Lanzarote's most photographed features. At close quarters the 'grape pits' do not look that impressive, but add a bit of altitude and how that perspective changes into an amazing landscape.

Originally a linear walk from **Uga** to **Puerto del Carmen**, we have now added an exciting circular option over **Montaña Tinasoria**, and an ascent of **Montaña de Guardilama** (not on windy days though). Now you can choose the option that suits you; either bus to **Yaiza** and do the linear walk to **Puerto del Carmen** (3 Walker), or follow the main walk to the pass and then climb **Tinasoria** as you curve back towards your outward route (4 Walker); to both of these you can add in the straight forward but tough ascent of **Guardilama** for its awesome views (5 Walker). No refreshments en-route, but there are bars in **Uga** and **Bar/Rest Gregorio** near our start point.

*Note that timings in the walk are given for the linear route direct to **Puerto del Carmen**.
For the ascent of **Guardilama** add 1 hour, 2.5 kilometres and 200 metres of ascents and descents.
For the ascent of **Tinasoria** add 40 minutes, 2.2 kilometres and 100 metres of ascents and descents.

> **Short Walk**
> **Tinasoria** Circular from **Uga**, ascending **Tinasoria** and then descending onto outward track. 3 Walker, 2 hours, 9.5 kilometres, Ascents/Descents 270 metres.

Our starting point is the from the bus stop by the church in **Uga** (Wp.1 0M), from where we walk (SE) down past the *dulceria* to the end of **Calle Jorge Rodriguez**. Going straight ahead, past cul-de-sacs left and right, we come up to a junction (Wp.2) where we go left along a narrow road. After a house on our right, we take a dirt road to the right which climbs steeply up to the **Teguise** road; alongside the track are our first examples of **La Geria** 'grape pits'. On the narrow main road we head away from **Uga** (NW) to take the first dirt road off to the right (Wp.3 17M).

Now we are into the **La Geria** grape growing area proper, though in these early stages there are more fields and terraces than the traditional grape vine *zocos* (depressions of volcanic ash enclosed in a horseshoe-shaped walled of volcanic rock with a vine planted in its centre). As we progress, the track runs along a plateau above **La Geria** for us to look across a landscape of *zocos* backed by the volcanic peaks of the **Timanfaya**.

... a landscape of *zocos* backed by the volcanic peaks of Timanfaya ...

Figs alternate with grapes as we climb steadily past a track off to the right, the **La Geria** landscape expanding into thousands of horseshoe-shaped depressions covering the whole region. Away on our left is one of the large *bodegas* as we continue uphill past the *bodega* access track (Wp.4) towards the pass. A steady, almost slogging, ascent brings us up onto the pass (Wp.5 57M) from where we can take a break for the views over the unique **La Geria** landscape. Now, if you think these views are impressive, think what another 100 or 200 metres altitude would do.

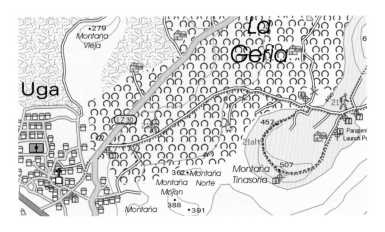

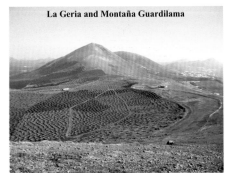
La Geria and Montaña Guardilama

Guardilama Option

If you are feeling fit and it's a calm day, then how about climbing **Guardilama** for the unforgettable views from its summit? Only attempt this on the calmest days as the wind sheer makes this route potentially dangerous. Not recommended for vertigo sufferers.

We go over the pass and in a few metres take a track to the left (Wp.6) to walk up past grapes enclosed by stone walls. After the last of the stone walls the track continues straight up the mountain. This truly is a 'puff and grunt' ascent, taking frequent breaks to get our breath back. The track peters out half way up, after which we follow a faint trail straight up over the open ground; another 50 metres of ascent and a few more stops for breath sees us reach the summit.

The views are simply awesome. **Guardilama** is Lanzarote's most 'pointy' accessible peak. The **La Geria** plain lies some 300 metres below us, and the views over the volcanic cones of the **Timanfaya** are unforgettable; stay as long as your vertigo will allow to enjoy the island's most spectacular views.

Take care on the steep descent, watching every step you make; it is all too easy to be distracted by the views and lose your footing on the steep ground.

Tinasoria Option (A less energetic, and easier option, than **Guardilama**)

From the pass we take a dirt road SW, to climb gently up between grape enclosures to come onto grass meadows, go left to the edge for impressive views down over **Puerto Calero**, and continue along the track to a graffiti-covered abandoned farm (Wp.7). The meadows in front of the farm are a popular *parapente* launch area where it is unusual not to see some hang-gliding taking place.

Continuing past the farm, our track gets rougher as we climb up the *lomo*, it is simply a case of slogging up the slope, either on the track which runs below the ridge line or on the ridge line itself, to a large stone cairn which marks the summit (Wp.8).

Though not quite as spectacular as from **Guardilama** (nothing is), but the views easily reward the small effort expended.

Tinasoria Circular

Tinasoria is not a peak in the 'pointy' sense, more a gentle hump. If we continue along the faint track (NW), now more traces than track, we see that it descends down the broad *lomo* as it curves round the crater floor. To make a circular route we simply follow the traces/track to come down to the flat ground where a better track takes us back onto our outward route. We then retrace our steps back to **Uga**.

Onward to Puerto del Carmen

From the pass we follow the dirt road down into the more familiar Lanzarote landscape, a steady descent bringing us down to a T-junction (Wp.9); **Camino del Mesón** track continuing ahead as we turn right to head downhill past a clutch of houses. We stay on the main track, passing a nice house and track on our left as we head down to cross the **Asomada** road (Wp.10 77M); there is a post at the junction, but its **Camino del Mesón** sign has gone missing.

Straight over the road, and we are back on a dirt track to come down past **Villa Vistas** to a crossroads of tracks (Wp.11) to continue straight over and come down onto a tarmac lane (Wp.12). Going right (S) we stroll down to the end of **Camino Los Olivos** to go left on a narrow lane and then right onto a track to carefully cross the fast and busy LZ2 main road.

We are back on a dusty track running down (SSE) through the general wasteland that lies between the mountains and the sea; a wasteland dotted with 'exclusively desirable villa residences' in local estate agent speak. At the end of **Camino La Caldarina** (Wp.13 97M) we take the track to the right (S) and at the next junction (Wp.14) we keep left to pass **Finca Lomos Altos** before reaching a T-junction where we go right to come onto the end of a tarmac lane (Wp.15) at another T-junction. Going left (E) passing a lane off to the left, and one to the right, we come to a lane off left to the main road. Keeping to our tarmac lane, we come to a second lane (Wp.16 120M) linking us to the **Puerto del Carmen** road.

If at this stage you are growing tired of the bungalow-dotted wasteland you could take to the main road for an easy tarmac stroll down to the *circunvalacion* roundabout, followed by pavements down into the resort.

The track down Barranco de Quiquere

Those of us choosing to stick with the grit head down (S) **Camino Barranco de Quiquere** past the multi-tiered garden of **Casa la Helice** for an easy stroll down past the grandly named little track of **Camino las Casanas** before coming onto the **Puerto Calero** road (Wp.17 138M). Straight over the road we continue on the track down to the mouth of the *barranco* where we meet the route of Walk 2 (Wp.18) From here we follow the coastal path (W) back to the 'old town' of **Puerto del Carmen** (172M).

Playa Quemada is literally the end of the road, but this doesn't mean that it's the end of exploring - far from it. Sections of this coastal exploration route get quite busy in a rather bizarre fashion, as the many people who head for the **Playa de la Arena** beach clad in the most minimalist gear contrast wildly with the *parapentes* who labour up to their launch point with enormous back packs. Once away from the first section of the route you are into barren tranquility, as we stroll above the cliffs before dropping into the large **Barranco de la Higuera** to find a few cozzie-optional hikers enjoying the isolated beach of **Playa del Pozo**.

3	2 H	5 km	⩓ 150m ⩔ 150m	⟺	0

Extension	Short Walk
This route can be extended into an ascent up to **Femés**, 7 Kilometres, Ascents 550 metres; see Walk 17.	To **Playa de la Arena** and return.

Access by car. Drive through **Playa Quemada** as far as you can. At the far end of the settlement keep left to come onto a cul-de-sac on the seaward side of the houses where there is parking for 8-10 cars.

The steep zigzag ascent

From beside the parking area (Wp.1 0M), a broad trail climbs up onto the headland to a cairn (Wp.2) above the first bay. This whole region is criss-crossed by a mixture of trails which can cause confusion, so we recommend staying on the main trail. Ahead, a clear trail zigzags up from the *barranco* behind **Playa la Arena** as we start curving into the *barranco* to a zigzag descent. Taking care on the slippery surface, we drop down to a path junction (Wp.3 8M) where most people go left and down to the **Playa de la Arena** beach. We continue straight on to climb the steep zigzag ascent onto the next headland; taking it one zig/zag at a time.

Our ascent brings us up to a T-junction (Wp.4 16M) whose right hand branch is an alternative return route avoiding the descent and ascent through the *barranco*. Going left we immediately hit another junction (Wp.5). Here the main path goes right to zigzag up the steep *lomo* to the *parapente* launch point, while we take the minor path straight ahead. We are now above the cliffs as we swing into a *barranco*, and ignoring a trace path descending, we stay on the narrow path to cross the *barranco*'s water runoff (Wp.6).

Coming out of the *barranco* the trace joins us and we have a choice of higher

or lower paths; it is quite amazing how this region has so many tracks and paths when it has not previously featured in any guide book.

Taking the higher path, we curve round into another *barranco*, and as our path runs out we find another couple of paths running into the *barranco*. In this myriad of traces we maintain altitude by stepping up onto the higher path off to our right (Wp.7 22M); our alternative return route winds inland, avoiding the steep ascents and descents by **Playa de la Arena**. Ignoring the many traces, we come along to cross the water runoff of the side *barranco* (Wp.8). We come out of the side *barranco* and immediately curve around the main *barranco* to finally emerge above the cliffs and azure sea. Our route is very much into and out of *barrancos* interspersed with sea views, as we cross yet another small *barranco* water runoff (Wp.9) and stay on the best defined path out of the *barranco* where our destination of **Playa del Pozo** comes into view (32M). It might look close, but there are still a few obstacles in the way. We turn into a small but precipitous *barranco* where the stone -littered path deserves careful footwork before crossing the water runoff (Wp.10). We come out of the small *barranco* to a choice of walking trail or dirt/stone track for our descent into the **Barranco de la Higuera**.

Across from us on the opposite wall of the *barranco* is an enormous stone design, a maritime anchor style design which was just being finished by the local sculptor when we were last on this route - if you look closely at the photo, you can just about make out the artist at the top right of his design. His presence gives a good impression of the size of his work.

Taking the walking trail, we descend until the path peters out and than transfer to the rubble-ised track. It looks as if we would have to go a long way up the *barranco,* but look for a walking trail leaving the track (Wp.11 40M). The narrow path drops us down towards the *barranco* floor, a cairn marking the last traverse (Wp.12) before we come onto a track (Wp.13) running along the *barranco* floor.

The refuge at Playa del Pozo

Going left, we follow the track to the mouth of the *barranco,* where it swings right behind the boulder beach to bring us across to the refuge (Wp.14 62M) and *pozo* from which the beach takes its name. There is little, if any, shade at **Playa del Pozo** so make sure you are well protected against the sun.

Our return is a retracing of our outward route until we reach the junction at Wp.7 (46M) where we keep straight on instead of dropping into the *barranco.* Our path runs inland, and as is the way of this area, a second path parallels our route twenty metres lower down the *barranco,* gently descending slopes covered with goat traces. We are heading towards a junction of barren valleys that conjoin inland of **Playa de la Arena**. At a faint junction (Wp.15) a trace goes ahead while our path turns right, its continuation is clearly seen across the valley, for us to join the second (lower) at the gravel lined water course. Now we have a steady ascent up the grit-surfaced path, easier to ascend than descend, to come onto a faint track (Wp.16) which runs along the *lomo.* We head back down the track towards the sea to rejoin our outward route.

> ## PLAYA DEL POZO
> It's thought that when the Normans invaded Lanzarote in 1402 under Jean de Béthencourt, the beach of **Playa del Pozo** became one of their first settlements. In the 1950s the Serra Ráfols brothers carried out archaeological investigations revealing the remains of a tower, a church, dwellings, wells, and a burial area. Other historians believe that the remains of the water channelling and well system, complete with triangular rock carvings, point to the Phoenicians as the first settlers. The *pozo* on the beach is a restoration of one of the original wells.

It's well worth strolling through this historic town, first established as a settlement by the island's original inhabitants, the *Mojos*. Cobbled streets lead between the white buildings, many of which have had a long and interesting history. You can visit the rather austere **Palacio Spinola** palace (open daily 10.00-17.00 in summer, until 09.00-15.00 in winter, entry fee payable) in the **Plaza de la Constitución**. There are several interesting churches, monasteries and museums worthy of a visit, including the prominent parish church, (16th century, but with numerous later embellishments) **Iglesia de Nuestra Señora de Guadalupe**, and the old **Teatrillo Municipal de Teguise** which first opened its doors in 1825. Most of the town's old buildings have changed use over the years, with many ex-convents and erstwhile homes of the rich and influential now serving as art galleries, museums, shops and bar/restaurants, while retaining their original façades. The town is at its busiest on Sunday mornings, when its street market acts as a magnet for both residents and visitors.

Overlooking the town on top of the peak of **Guanapay** (446 metres) perches the island's oldest castle, the **Castillo de Santa Bárbara**. This fortress was built in the 16th century, but became seriously dilapidated until it was rescued and restored in order to house the **Museo del Emigrante Canario** which specialises in artefacts marking the history of migration by Lanzarote's inhabitants in their attempts to find fortune overseas, mainly in South America. Enjoy the panoramic views from the peak, or take a look inside (€3 adults, 10.00-16.00 Mon-Fri, 10.00-15.00 Sun).

Although we suggest a route, you may wish to stroll around this compact old town centre in a less formal manner by referring to the street plan.

N.B. We have not included GPS information for this walk, as satellite coverage in the narrow streets is unreliable.

Access by car: Parking in the **Plaza Spinola** and along the main road.

Access by bus: In addition to the Sunday market day specials (Nºs 11, 12&13), Nºs 7, 9&10 all go via **Teguise**.

Whether you arrive by car or bus, you might wish to begin this relaxed stroll with refreshments in one of the town's bars. If you arrive early, then call in the **Sejas Bar/Café** in **Plaza Doctor Alfonso Spínola** (open from 06.00 until 20.00), which backs onto the old **Convento de San Francisco** (1534), no longer used as a convent, but housing Lanzarote's collection of religious art in the **Museo de Arte Sacro**. Leaving the bar, we turn right and walk through the *plaza,* named after the Teguise-born Doctor Spinola (1845-1905) who was a medical doctor in Lanzarote and also in Uruguay, where he was important in controlling a smallpox outbreak. Turning right at the north-east corner brings us onto **Calle Marqués de Herrera**, passing the **Casa del Marqués** on our left, and continuing on the few steps past the narrow street on our left to see the **Teatrillo Municipal de Teguise** which has given service as a church, hospital and children's hospice before becoming a theatre in 1825.

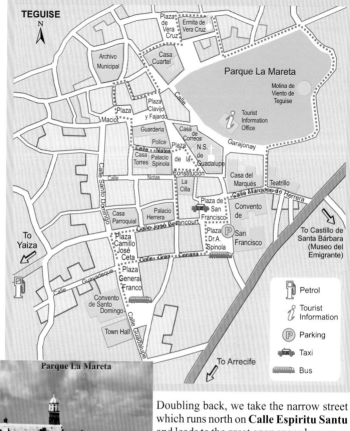

TEGUISE
N

Plaza de Vera Cruz
Ermita de Vera Cruz
Archivo Municipal
Casa Cuartel
Parque La Mareta
Molina de Viento de Teguise
Plaza Clavijo y Fajardo
Calle
Plaza Maciot
Guarderia
Tourist Information Office
Casa de Correos
Police
Plaza N.S. de de Guadalupe
Garajonay
Calle Notas
Casa Torres
Palacio Spinola
Constitución
Casa del Marqués
Teatrillo
Calle Santo Domingo
Calle
Notas
La Cilla
Calle Marques de Herrera
Plaza de San Francisco
Convento de
Casa Parroquial
Palacio Herrera
Calle José Betancourt
Plaza Dr.A. Spinola
San Francisco
To Castillo de Santa Bárbara (Museo del Emigrante)
To Yaiza
Plaza Camillo José Ceta
Calle Gran Canaria
Plaza General Franco
Calle Guayadeque
Calle Guadalupe
Convento de Santo Domingo
Town Hall
To Arrecife

To Yaiza

Petrol

Tourist Information

Parking

Taxi

Bus

Parque La Mareta

Doubling back, we take the narrow street which runs north on **Calle Espiritu Santu** and leads to the great open space known as **Parque La Mareta**, although there is little evidence of greenery in this large public area. If you are fortunate enough to be on the island on June 1, this square is transformed by colourful 'carpets' drawn with coloured salts.

Following its edge counter-clockwise brings us to a well preserved (except for some graffiti) windmill **Molino de Viento de Teguise**, the last remaining one of twelve in this area which were used to grind cereal grains. We continue our circumnavigation of the *parque*, turning off north on the **Calle Princesa Ico** and into **Plaza de Vera Cruz** dominated by the **Ermita de Vera Cruz** with its magnificently huge doors. Leaving the *plaza* by its south-west corner, we walk to the next junction of streets where we go

El Molino de Viento de Teguise

Casa Cuartel

left (S), passing the **Casa Cuartel** on our left which formerly provided billets for soldiers, easily recognised by its old wooden balcony - there are very few of these on this largely treeless island.

Continuing ahead and taking a short dogleg right and left brings us into **Plaza de Clavijo y Fajardo**, where we turn right on a narrow street, at the end of which the **Archivo Municipal** faces us. Turning left and immediately left again brings us into **Plaza Maciot**, which we walk through to leave by the narrow street in its south-east corner, then taking the next left with **Casa Torres** forming the corner, next door to the seventeenth century **Palacio Spínola** which became a museum in 1984, its walls on this side in the **Calle Notas** looking rather unstable, although the palace is considered to be the most important building (architecturally) in the town. We step out into the main cobbled square of **Plaza de la Constitución**, the main façade and entrance to **Palacio Spínola** on its western side, and with the **Iglesia de Nuestra Señora de Guadalupe** on the opposite side. It is an imposing building, standing out amongst the rather austere and simple architectural styles of much of the town. On the north side of the church is a building that once served as the post office, still known as the **Casa de Correos** but now used by the Univerity of Las Palmas de Gran Canaria as a School of Medicine. By the south side of the church, the narrow lane **Calle Zonzamas** leads into the **Parque La Mareta**.

Cilla de Diezmos y Primicias

Also look for the seventeenth century **Caja Canarias**, on the southern edge of the square, one of the most attractive banks you are likely to see, housed in the **Cilla de Diezmos y Primicias** building once used to store grain paid as tithes - not too much of a change of use, then.

We leave the *plaza* by the street at its south-west corner, **Calle Leon y Castillo**, taking the second right onto **Calle José Betancort**, bringing us past the **Palacio Herrera** on our right - turn right around the building's corner to see its impressive wall plaque set into the wall, before retracing our steps back onto **Calle José Betancort** and continue in a westerly direction, passing the **Casa Paroquial** on our right. Turning left at the end of the street where it meets **Calle Guadalupe** at **Plaza Camillo José Cela** takes us past a small public garden and bus stop, opposite the **Convento de Santo Domingo** (1698), one of the town's largest buildings, and an important centre for local government offices and cultural activities in this region. It also houses the **Centro de Arte Santo Domingo** (open Mon-Fri 10.00 - 15.00, Sun 10.00-14.00). To return to our start point, backtrack to the first street right, **Calle Gran Canaria**, which leads us back to **Plaza Doctor Alfonso Spínola**.

24. THE FORGOTTEN TRAIL

If there is one route that you should walk on Lanzarote, this is it. Our route contains all the essentials for a top rate discovery and even the 280 metre ascent simply melts away as we climb a little known donkey trail through the lushest vegetation on the island.

Originally a linear descent to **Haría**, we've now re-walked the route as an 'out and back' excursion, with basic refreshments being taken at half way.

Short Route
Take a taxi to **Bar/Rest Los Helechos** and walk the route as a linear descent to **Haría**.

Stroll
Along the dirt road from **Haría**, as far as you like.

We start out from the centre of **Haría** outside **Bar Ney-Ha** on the **Plaza de la Constitución** (Wp.1 0M) to go right in front of the *ayuntamiento* to stroll along to the **Ekog** collection shop (Wp.2) where we go left on a small street lined with houses. It is gently uphill before going left to cross the stream bed and come up past a well (Wp.3) to a T-junction at the end of **Calle Angel**. Following the 'Deportivo' sign to the right, we start leaving the old village behind as we stroll along an avenue of palms. Fields replace houses on our left as we pass the César Manrique house (Wp.4) on our right, shortly before the tarmac swings right (Wp.5) towards the sports complex. Here we continue

straight ahead, the tarmac changing to dirt (Wp.6 12M) as we pass a ruined cottage to finally leave the housing behind.

Ahead, the line of the donkey trail which climbs the ridge at the end of the valley is clearly visible, the buildings on top of the ridge making for a rather daunting prospect from down in the valley. We stroll along through a bucolic landscape of black *picon* cultivated plots interspersed with fallow fields populated with endemic flora.

Coming to a junction (Wp.7) we take the minor dirt road to our front right. Our gentle uphill stroll becomes more serious as the road steepens, becoming grassier as it ascends in a slogging ascent towards the main road. Where the dirt road swings left up to the tarmac we take a donkey trail straight ahead to climb up onto the road (Wp.8 27M).

Watching out for 'white knuckled' hire car drivers, we cross over onto the donkey trail's continuation on a long traverse across the slope. Endemic flora has narrowed the trail to path width as we climb up above a cultivated black *picon* plot which stands out amongst these long-abandoned terraces. At the end of the long climbing traverse, we come up to meet the main road again (Wp.9 40M) by the 'Val de Malpaiso' sign.

Surrounded by plant life, far above Haría

Carefully over the road we continue on the donkey trail in another climbing traverse, the plant growth on this steep hillside simply has to be seen to be believed; if you think of Lanzarote as 'grit and desert' then this floriferous setting will really surprise you. Giant sonchus, lavender, succulents and tamarisk cling to every available roothold.

A boulder-cobbled section of the trail

A slogging ascent brings us up under massive buttresses which support the road, as a hairpin bend in the trail (Wp.10 43M) directs us towards another buttress. We come up to touching distance of the massive wall to zigzag steeply up alongside the tarmac (Wp.11) at a hairpin bend.

Our trail is mostly boulder-cobbled now, as we climb steeply up through more zigzags to a hairpin bend (Wp.12) that directs us towards the **Mirador de Haría** building, a climbing traverse leading us up to the road again (Wp.13 48M).

Carefully crossing the road, we find our trail's continuation 20 metres uphill where the path climbs up from a red rock dell, soon becoming boulder-laid again. As our trail curves right, we get views down the **Valle de Tenisía** as we push our way up through lush plant life to come up to the road again.

From here you could simply walk up the road to the Bar/Restaurant, but we cross the road to come onto the faintest section of the trail. Above us is a wooden cross which we use as a direction marker while climbing up over bare rock, before the trail resumes to take us past the cross (Wp.14). Twenty metres after the cross there is faint (easily missed) junction (Wp.15 55M), where our 'Capital Route' continues gently uphill to come onto a dirt road. At the junction we go left, to drop down the cobbled trail to the road (Wp.16).

Now we have an uphill stroll beside the crash barrier to turn into **Bar/Rest Los Helechos** (62M 570 metres), which may look closed from the roadside - but walk around the building to find a twee gift shop selling the usual tourist stuff, and a large basic café geared up for the coach potato trade. It doesn't rate highly for refreshments, but it is a reasonably comfortable place to take a break and mix with the tourists and groups of lycra-clad cyclists who call in here.

We return by retracing our outward route, taking care on the steeper stretches of the donkey trail which can become very slippery in bad weather.

25. CIRCUIT OF HARÍA

The region around **Haría** contains quite a diversity of landscapes, ranging from lush valleys to barren hills and an unusual custom built *mirador* that nobody seems to know about. Our route is a complete mixture of a little tarmac, quite a lot of dirt road, a steep climb, a pathless section, breathtaking views; and the pleasure that comes from knowing that you will not have to share any of this with coach potatoes.

Access by car: Park in **Haría**.

<table>
<tr><td>

Stroll

From the **Ekog** collection shop continue westwards on the street, which becomes the dirt road running up the valley to the *mirador* and return the same way.

</td><td>

Short Walk

Follow the route in reverse to the *mirador*, then continue on the dirt road back into **Haría**.

</td></tr>
</table>

We start in the centre of **Haría** opposite **Bar Ney-Ha** (Wp.1 0M). Our first objective is the road junction at the top of the town. We can either walk straight up the **Máguez** road (N), or take the pedestrian street (E) past the church and then turn left (N) up the street; both options are the least pleasant part of the route as we slog up narrow streets. Both routes climb up the northern summit of the town, coming together (Wp.2) at a junction from which we head out on a country road on our front left (NE); the **Calle Casa Atras**, rather a grand name for a smear of tarmac laid on a dirt road. Leaving

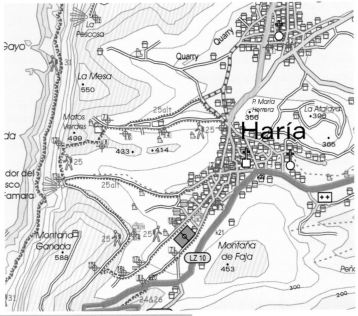

the houses behind, we have views across the valley to a large quarry as we stroll down to a junction with a dirt road (Wp.3) going left (E).

Here we go left on the dirt road, but you could continue down the tarmac into the valley to go left on the next dirt road; a slightly longer and more energetic choice though, and with less extensive views. It's an easy stroll across the southern slope of the valley, passing through a patchwork of neatly cultivated plots and fallow fields being reclaimed by endemic plants. We stroll past a squat house (Wp.4) surrounded by cultivated plots, and the dirt road becomes less used as we head up the valley. A steep dirt road drops down to the right linking our route with the longer alternative (Wp.5) before we crest a rise and our road runs gently downhill to a junction with the alternative route (Wp.6). It is noticeable that the valley's southern slopes are more lush than the northern and mostly barren slopes, as we steadily ascend to come up to a breeze-block walled enclosure (Wp.7 33M).

Here we have another choice of route, our official route taking the faint track that climbs steeply up beside the enclosure. Another option is to continue on the dirt road to its end and follow a steep trail up over **Matos Verdes** to join our official route below the peak. The problem with this cliff top route is that it is usually extremely windy on all but the calmest days.

The summit of the ridge, 40 minutes into the route

We take the faint track and start climbing steeply - and we do mean steeply - as the slope would benefit from having stairs cut into it. A 'puff and grunt' ascent takes us up past the top of the enclosure to reach the summit of the ridge by a gap in a stone wall (Wp.8 40M). After that exertion you have an excuse to stop and take in the extensive views over the **Haría** valley before continuing

Once through the wall, we swing right to follow it uphill towards a sad and lonely palm, the path is so little used we could think of this section as 'open ground' navigation. A small cairn (Wp.9) marks the spot where we move away from the wall and start to cross the long abandoned terraces to another gap in another stone wall (Wp.10). **La Caleta** and **Famara** come into view - and what a view it is - as we cross the terraces to a gap in another stone wall (Wp.11).

The path at 52 minutes

As we round the slopes below **Matos Verdes** we maintain altitude as we pass above a large stone storm-water wall which protects the lower valley, before coming to a path (Wp.12) 52M) which runs down from the peak along the top of the cliffs; you'll notice that the wind's strength is multiplied several fold here near the cliff edge. We pick our way down the path's gritty surface, which improves as we get lower, but it's still wiser to stop if you want to take in the impressive views. Our route runs down to join a dirt road beside an unusual structure (Wp.13 60M).

From above, this roofless structure resembles a very fancy grape vine cultivator, but from close to it is clearly a series of windbreaks for picnickers, along with a parking area, so that they can enjoy the *mirador* views with some protection from the high winds; rather a shame that it does not feature on maps or in guide books, as visitors are very unlikely to stumble across this stunning location. While at the *mirador*, take the opportunity to look down the cliffs where you'll see that there is a clear path cut across the cliff-face; this is part of our Walk 31 'Risco de Famara' route.

From the *mirador* you have a choice of either short cutting down the dirt road running down the valley to **Haría**, or taking our official longer route exploring the **Haría** valley. Leaving the *mirador*, we head up the dirt road which runs below the slopes of **Montaña Ganada**.

Views over the Haría valley as we descend

After a steady uphill, the gradient eases for easy strolling between abandoned terraces above and below our route as more of **Haría** comes into sight ahead of us. A pungent whiff announces a goat farm ahead as we pass the first cultivated plots, climbing a rise before the road turns right above the goat farm (Wp.14 74M), giving excellent views over the **Haría** valley.

Now we have easy strolling towards **Valle de Malpaso**, our route lined with gigantic prickly pear in places as we walk above neatly cultivated plots to come to a junction (Wp.15 80M). Going left, we leave the main dirt track to descend between the plots on a rough track, once a boulder-laid donkey trail but now much eroded and covered in *picon* grit in places, requiring careful footwork on our descent. The track narrows to a trail and then to a path, before it comes down to a track which runs along the valley floor (Wp.16 88M).

Gratefully, we turn left and head along the track as it runs gently downhill to come onto a better stabilised track by a chained entrance (Wp.17 91M). It's comfortable strolling, crossing a plant-choked water course before we reach civilisation in the form of the sports centre football ground (Wp.18), after which the houses start. Continuing down the tarmac street we turn right at its end, by the **Ekog** collection shop, and walk along to the **Plaza de la Constitución** and the prospect of an *agua con gas* followed by a cold beer in **Bar Ney-Ha** (110M).

26. CAPITAL ROUTE - HARÍA TO TEGUISE

In far distant days **Teguise** was the capital of Lanzarote, and as is the way of things, all routes led to the capital. This long linear route is a relic of those times, when it provided the main route from **Haría** to the capital. Being a ridge-top route, it has survived the depredations of road building largely intact, and its elevation produces many spectacular views. There is a stiff climb through Lanzarote's most floriferous landscape, but you can divert to **Bar/Rest Los Helechos** for refreshments after completing most of the ascent. Once on the ridge - more a wide-backed *lomo* - it's easy striding with stops to take in the awesome cliff-top views. After those views, trailing down into **Teguise** is rather disappointing, but at least it makes for easy walking.

Access by Bus: Nº7 from **Arrecife**.

Short Walk.
See Walk 24, 'The Forgotten Trail'

We start out from the centre of **Haría**, following the directions for 'The Forgotten Trail', up to Wp.15 (55M). If, with most of the ascent behind you,

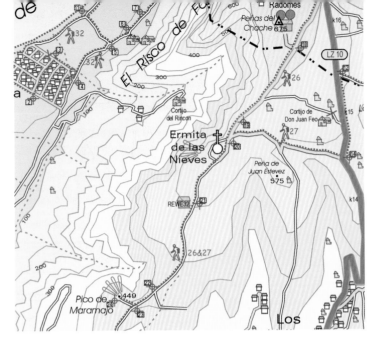

you want to take a break, then follow 'The Forgotten Trail' road walk up to **Bar/Rest Los Helechos**. On leaving the bar, walk south along the road and take the first tarmac lane off to the right to meet our official route just before the military radar golf-balls.

From Wp.15 we continue straight ahead to come onto a dirt road. Keeping straight on along the track, we come up past a house, with **Bar/Rest Los Helechos** across a field on our left. We walk up past two more houses, the radar golf-balls coming into sight, before a section of the track goes left while we continue onto the tarmac lane (Wp.16) which serves the **Ermita de las Nieves**. We have an easy stroll along the narrow lane, ignoring a track to our front right (Wp.17), and passing the radar station entrance (Wp.18), with views opening up to our left (E) over the main road and down to the coastal plain.

Over a small crest, and now the *ermita* comes into view ahead of us. This is easy striding country, so you might care to divert right to a *mirador* viewpoint at the top of the cliffs (Wp.19) before strolling over to arrive at the *ermita*'s walled courtyard (Wp.20 90M), where we take shelter from the wind inside its walled garden.

The pilgrims' well in the *ermita*'s garden

From the **Ermita de las Nieves,** our route could not be more straightforward. We simply stroll south-west on the dirt road, passing 'REWE32' (Wp.21),

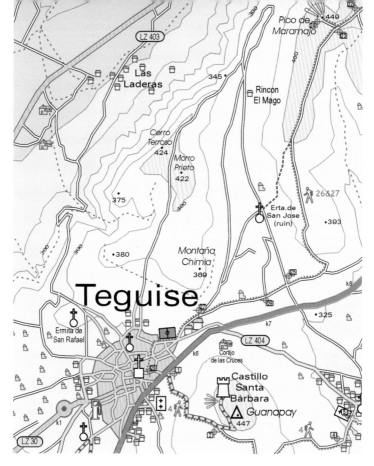

another military compound with aerials. The dirt road, little used by vehicles, makes for easy strolling as it runs gently downhill along the broad backed *lomo*.

... views, views ...

Whenever we feel the need for more imposing views we can always divert right to the cliff top. We pass a track off to the left (Wp.22) before coming to a junction (Wp.23) where we go right to a *mirador* viewpoint overlooking a sharp cleft in the cliffs (Wp.24); beautiful views and even equipped with seat-height rocks to relax on.

We come back to the main track to continue gently downhill with the **Castillo de Santa Bárbara** dominating the view ahead. Our route curves towards the south and the first buildings of **Teguise** come into view. A black *picon* field stands out against the barren landscape, just before we have a small uphill section, after which the track starts to run down off the *lomo* towards a patchwork of cultivated fields. Our track curves down to a cross-roads of tracks (Wp.25).

The main road is away on our left as we go straight ahead on the narrower track running between the plots directly towards the town. We pass a track off to the right (Wp.26) before strolling up behind the first buildings of the town at a track junction (Wp.27) then reaching the football ground (Wp.28) where we finally come onto town streets. Keeping the church tower as our direction finder we stroll down the quiet streets (on weekdays at least) to arrive in the main square (Wp.29).

ERMITA DE LAS NIEVES

The **Ermita de las Nieves** (The Chapel of the Snows) stands in isolation at Lanzarote's coldest spot, its exposed position also subjecting it to frequent batterings by relentless winds. Thankfully, then, visitors can take shelter inside its surrounding walls, an oasis of relative calm away from the ferocity of the elements within which a garden thrives.

The building of the *ermita* began in the 17th century, but has been added to over the years, giving it a relatively modern appearance. It has been a pausing point for pilgrims of all sorts over the centuries, whether seeking spiritual sustenance or the quenching of thirst from its drinking water supply, though we can't vouch for its potability. The *ermita* itself is open on Saturdays (14.30 -18.00) and on 5th August, its saint's day.

The Ermita de las Nieves

Views over Famara from the cliff edge

The views from the cliffs near the *ermita* shouldn't be missed, but take great care, especially on windy days (unfortunately, in the majority). **Playa de Famara** lies below, while the island of **La Graciosa** will be visible on a clear day to your right, beyond the **Risco de Famara** cliff.

You may also make out the further islands of **Montaña Clara** and beyond that, **Isla de Alegranza** when the visibility allows. The highest point on the island (670 metres), **Peñas del Chache**, stands out to the north-north east, seventy metres higher than the *ermita*. This vantage point is occupied by a military installation, and is off limits to visitors.

Another of Lanzarote's classic walking routes, all of which is on well stabilised dirt tracks or tarmac. The second half of the route, from **Ermita de las Nieves**, is common to Walks 26 and 27; so it is not repeated again here. Our route has been only marginally affected by the new LZ1 road opened in March 2004 as our original track is now bridged over the new fast road. Our personal preference is for our **Haría-Teguise** route as the initial ascent simply melts away, but here it is always staring you in the face all the way up to the ridge. If you have an old Noel Rochford Landscapes (1998 edition) and a GPS, this is a good route to compare modern navigation techniques with a pre-GPS description.

Access by Bus: N°9, and some of the N°7 buses to **Mala**; alight at the *farmacía*, then walk along the old main road (N) for 200 metres and just past the village school our route starts at the tarmac lane on the left (Wp.1).

Access by Car: Not really a car drivers route except by our '2CSK' approach. Park off the old main road in **Mala**, but on the main road in **Teguise**; it is easier to find a car on the main road than in the warren of town streets.

Before starting out, it's a good idea to make sure we are equipped for this energetic ascent up to the ridge. It's a long ascent of 2 hours plus and 600 metres, climbing almost every step of the way after a deceptively easy start. If you doubt your fitness, try routes 24 and 26 first.

> **Short Walk**
> To **Ermita de las Nieves** and return (3½ hours) and you get the benefit from your climb on the downhill return.

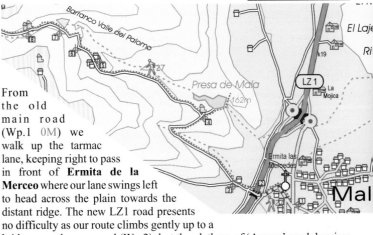

From the old main road (Wp.1 0M) we walk up the tarmac lane, keeping right to pass in front of **Ermita de la Merceo** where our lane swings left to head across the plain towards the distant ridge. The new LZ1 road presents no difficulty as our route climbs gently up to a bridge over the new road (Wp.2), but the plethora of 'Armco' crash barriers and new wide dirt roads has ruined a once tranquil landscape. Over the bridge, and we are heading towards rural tranquility as we come up to a pair of houses

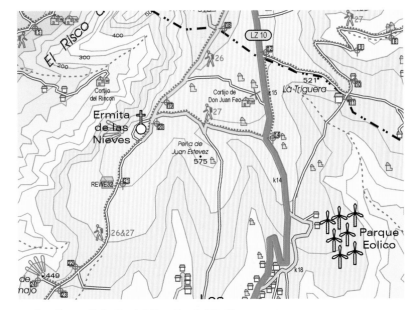

at a junction and take the right hand track (Wp.3).

Cochineal farming

We are now climbing steadily up the side of a valley to go through a hairpin bend across its watercourse which gives us views back over our outward route, and the fields devoted to the 'tunera' cactus and their 'crop' of Cochineal beetle which are still cultivated in this region.

We come up onto the line of the ridge and a junction beside a ruin (Wp.4 26M) where a track goes off to our right. There is still plenty of climbing to come, so you might want to take a break by walking out along the track to see the **Presa de Mala** dam, only containing water after wet weather.

From the *presa* junction we continue up the track toward a distant hamlet, the ground around our route deeply scarred by storm water erosion, in contrast to the massively walled terraces along this section. A steady ascent brings us up to the hamlet (Wp.5 44M) to walk past an impressive stone wall (Wp.6) and the radomes come into view; known locally as the 'golf balls'. With the cliff wall at the head of the **Barranco Valle del Palomo** looming ahead of us, we start slicing our route up into our 'one step after another' approach with a dam in the *barranco* floor (Wp.7) giving us the chance for a 'Look at that' breather. Passing a ruin (Wp.8) gives another excuse, as does a small bridge (Wp.9 71M). Cultivated plots enclosed by well built walls have relieved the ascent so far, but there is no denying that it is uphill and more uphill as our track zigzags up for us to reach a small house with an interesting back garden (Wp.10 88M).

At last the gradient eases as we come up to a white building set alongside a five-way junction (Wp.11) to the north of the **Parque Eólico** wind farm. Turning right to pass in front of the building, we have the luxury of a gentle uphill stroll to come onto the LZ10 road (Wp.12 105M), facing the radomes set on **Peñas del Chache**. Turning left down the road we head towards the wind farm to take the lane on the right (Wp.13) signed to the **Ermita de las Nieves**. Up the lane, we wriggle through a zigzag before coming up to meet the dirt track of Walk 26 (Wp.14). Left up the tarmac, or around the dirt track that runs around the western side, brings us up to a well earned break at the island's best known *ermita* (Wp.15 132M).

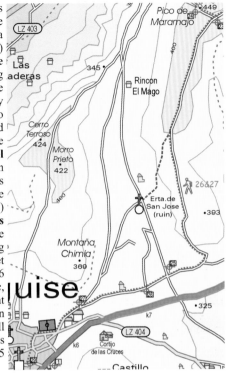

Famara and La Caleta, far below

Ermita de las Nieves (Chapel of the Snows) is a popular stopping off point for both walkers and drivers, and could be idyllic, if only someone would put in a little *tipico* bar to cater for the many visitors. Sitting on the well in the *ermita*'s courtyard is the most comfortable option, but we would not rely upon the well's water supply. If you have made the climb in hot weather (What other sort is there on Lanzarote?) you will appreciate the cool shade given by the courtyard walls. Before leaving, stroll west across the parking area to the edge of the escarpment for the best views down over **Famara** and **La Caleta**.

Our second stage of the route into **Teguise** is identical to Walk 26. GPS users should note that waypoints 16 to 23 are equivalent to waypoints 21 to 28 of Walk 26.

Also note that the GPS waypoints are not identical, having been recorded on different days in very slightly different positions; (see page 22).

This interesting circular route takes in bucolic farmland, upland meadows (yes, meadows), stunning cliff-top views, a peak and one of Lanzarote's most impressive *calderas*; only refreshments are missing. Ascents are never steeper than steady, and the range of landscapes and views makes even these seem relatively gentle. All the route is on either narrow tarmac lanes or well-stabilised dirt tracks, so you could drive this route - but why you would want to?

Some guides describe the main circuit of this route in the opposite direction. This involves a mind-sapping relentless ascent right from the start which makes the route seem more penance than enjoyment.

Short route
Omit the four diversions off the main circuit, but you will miss some of the most interesting features.
Alternative Short Route
Park just off the **Guinate** road by Wp.6 and follow official route to Wp.9 and go right to return to your car - see map.

Stroll
Drive up the route in reverse and make the ascent of **Helechos** on foot

Access by car with on street parking in **Máguez**, possibly by bus on route N°7.

We start off in the centre of **Máguez** by house number 16 (Wp.1 0M) by going (ENE) along a quiet street past the church on our left to come along to a cross roads (Wp.2) where we go left. A steady uphill stroll takes us past houses and vegetable plots, with **Helechos** on our front left. The street gets steeper and narrower before we go over the crest to leave **Calle las Casillas** on a well-used dirt track (Wp.3). After that steepish urban start we are now heading out (NE) into a bucolic landscape with the bulk of **Monte Corona** ahead of us. This is easy strolling between fallow and cultivated plots, passing tracks off to right and left, before coming to a junction (Wp.4) where we go left on the minor track.

Our track gently climbs past a rock outcrop towards a pair of buildings. The buildings resolve into a house and its garage as we come to the crest of the track to see the main road and **Guinate** junction ahead of us. Another easy stroll down through a meadow landscape (yes, this *is* Lanzarote) brings us to the main road opposite the **Mirador de Guinate** road (Wp.5).

Along the **Guinate** road, we turn off the tarmac onto a track (Wp.6). Now it is a steady climb round the slopes of **Helechos**, the effort partly relieved by the expanding views as we ascend past ancient walls and long abandoned plots. Past a cultivated field and a lichen-encrusted outcrop announces our arrival at a pass (453 metres) and a few metres further (Wp.7) we take a diversion to our right to follow a faint track (NW) to a viewpoint (Wp.8) at a stone wall

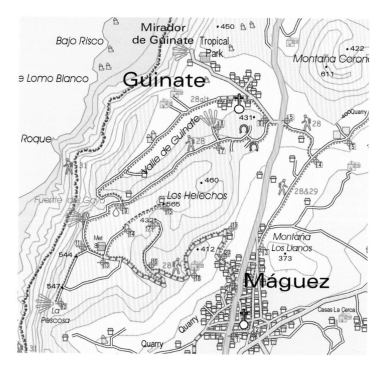

overlooking the **Guinate** valley. Just beyond the wall, stone-walled, black *picon* plots of grape vines contrast with the meadows we have crossed.

The purple sheen of Viper's-bugloss

Back on the main track (Wp.7) we head up (WSW) through the waving grassland and meadow flowers towards another pass. Viper's-bugloss flowers give the slopes a gentle purple sheen as we come up to overlook the **Valle de Guinate**: the dirt road running along the valley is the route of our Alternative Short Walk. Now we stroll along overlooking the valley beside fallow meadow fields. On our front right is a remarkable 'bite' out of the ridge as though bitten by giant teeth; yes, you <u>could</u> drive this route, but how much more enjoyable to stroll through this wonderful landscape.

An uphill section takes us up past a house to a junction (Wp.9), where our Alternative Short Route goes right to drop down towards the valley floor.

Just past the junction we pass a pair of pits beside the track before reaching a Y-junction where we take the left fork; the two tracks soon coming together again. A valley drops steeply down on our right as we continue uphill to the top of the cliffs (Wp.10); take care if you approach the cliff edge as the winds are powerful. We stay on the track as it undulates along (SE) away from the cliffs to reach a junction (Wp.11). Here we take the minor track (WSW) heading for the cliff tops at **La Pescosa**. We walk up past fields cut out of the meadows to come up onto the headland. This track ends at a storm-eroded area (Wp.12) from where we take in impressive views down over **El Risco de Famara** to **La Caleta** and the plain beyond.

Back at the main track (Wp.11) we head (E) past a white meteorological station, where the track becomes tarmacked, to another junction (Wp.13) where a track goes left (N). Taking to the track for our third diversion off the main circular route, we climb up onto a broad backed ridge which although only a few metres above our earlier route is almost barren with the exception of a black *picon* field. We walk along the rough track to swing left and right beside the field (Wp.14).

David just visible on the Helechos peak track

Ahead, the track leads us up the slope to the transmitter hut sitting on the top of **Helechos**, views opening up down over the **Valle de Guinate** from the saddle before the final walk up to the hut (Wp.15). The rounded summit has plenty of plant life and the wreck of a transmitting tower blown down by ferocious winds. This is literally the high point of our route, so take your time enjoying the panoramic views before returning to our main route.

The *caldera* below Helechos peak

Back on the tarmac (Wp.13) we head (E) downhill, steadily at first and then steeply down through a hairpin bend to a junction (Wp.16) where a track heads off towards the **Helechos** peak from the second hairpin bend. By now you might well be dreaming of a cold beer in **Máguez** and be tempted to ignore this track, but stay with us for our fourth, and final, diversion off the main route. We walk out along the track, which is nothing special until it reaches a crest for us to find ourselves looking down into the *caldera* directly below the **Helechos** peak.

Our track continues down around the wall of the crater to reach the flat floor at the foot of sheer cliffs (Wp.17), giving us an impressive sense of scale in this soaring cliff landscape despite some rubbish dumping. Climbing back up the track out of the *caldera*, we arrive back at the tarmac. Now the return to **Máguez** is straightforward, as we simply walk down the tarmac lane, descending past cultivated fields, a farm (Wp.18) and an unusual dwelling set below the road (Wp.19). Houses start (Wp.20) shortly before we meet the main road (Wp.21) where we go right to walk down to our start point.

A pleasing rural route, giving close up views of Lanzarote's agricultural region seldom seen by the average visitor. The range of different landscapes encountered on this moderate length route has to be seen to be believed. All the walking is on good dirt tracks or tarmac, technically driveable but much more fun on foot.

3 | 2½ H | 10 km | 240m / 170m | 2*

*in the **Centro Social Cultural de Yé**

Access by Bus: Route Nº7 serves both **Máguez** and **Yé**, but not all departures call at **Yé**. See timetables for details.

Short Route

Park at **Yé** and walk back down the road (SE) until you come to the dirt track at Wp.7, then follow the main description for a circular route of 6.5 kilometres.

Starting from the centre of **Máguez** we follow the same route as Walk 28, 'Helechos Circular' until that route turns left at Wp.4.

At this junction we keep straight ahead (NE) on the main track to walk gently uphill, as the bulk of **Monte Corona** starts to loom over us. Passing a water tank with blue door we come over a

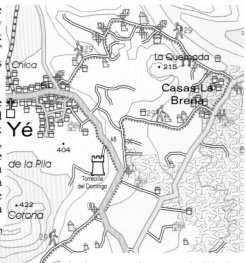

rise by a second water tank (Wp.5) to come into a *picon* landscape, much harsher than the earlier plain. Sturdy boulder walls criss-cross the land ahead as we pass a *picon* quarry, very different to the cultivated fields away on our right.

As our track wriggles through the moonscape, the top of the large mansion of **Torrecilla de Domingo** comes into view, gradually exposing itself as we come alongside cultivated plots and keep left at a junction just before meeting the main road (Wp.6).

Torrecilla de Domingo

Uphill, on or alongside the tarmac, we pass in front of the mock-fortified mansion of **Torrecilla de Domingo** to leave the road on a broad track (Wp.7) that drops down between stone walls. We head out into a 'walled' landscape - and we really do mean walled, as it seems as though there are more walls than you would ever need to protect crops, not that this can any longer be a consideration as the whole area is long abandoned.

We stay on the main track, passing two tracks off right before coming over a rise, where the landscape ahead becomes more normal with cultivated plots. Strolling down the track, we pass a weekender cottage followed by cultivated *picon*-covered plots and houses as our route runs down to the **Orzola** road (Wp.8).

Going left (NE) we stroll down the road to take a track (Wp.9) off to the left that curves around behind a clutch of modern houses. Our route climbs up towards the twin peaks of **Montaña Quemada** which we pass on our left as the track rises up to overlook the **Vega Grande** valley. With the views comes a stiff uphill section of the track, stone-walled on our left and with a steep drop on our right, which lasts until we reach the saddle at an art-deco house (Wp.10).

Views over the Vega Grande valley

Over the saddle, we ignore a minor track left as we head down above cultivated fields in the valley below us, passing an old mill (Wp.11) and a ruin beside interesting rocks (Wp.12) before reaching the cultivated fields which stretch up the valley on our right. Passing a track off to the left (Wp.13) and one off to the right (Wp.14), we face a stiff climb up from the valley floor, passing another two tracks off to the left before the gradient eases beside

The Centro Socio de Yé

walled grape vines. Passing a house on our left, we walk steadily uphill in a slogging ascent to the first houses of **Yé** (Wp.15) where we turn left to meet the main road. Do call in at the most unusual *tipico* bar on the island in the **Centro Socio Cultural de Yé** alongside the main bus stop, for coffee and to admire the murals.

Yé is a sleepy farming village far removed from the excesses of Lanzarote's beach resorts. In addition to its rural tranquility, it boasts the most unusual *tipico* bar on the island in the **Centro Socio Cultural de Yé** alongside the main bus stop; do call in for coffee and admire the wall murals. Most visitors who discover **Yé** are simply passing through on their way to the 'pay on entry' sanitised **Mirador del Río**; once a simple gun emplacement dating from the civil war, but now upgraded to a 'tourist' attraction for the coach potatoes.

Less well known, and largely undiscovered by the casual visitor, is the *mirador* overlooking the **Salinas del Río** where you will not only enjoy similar views, but you'll be in the unusual situation of seeing your whole walking route laid out in front of you before you start out. Even if you do not plan to walk the **Salinas del Río**, or the 'Yé to La Caleta' cliff-face walk, you must visit this *mirador* if your visit to Lanzarote is to be complete.

Access by Car: From **Maguez**, drive past the **Guinate** junction, and turn off the main road 1.7 kilometres further on, onto a narrow lane at **Las Rositas**. Drive carefully down the lane until the imposing **Finca La Corona** is on your right, and then turn left onto a stone-flagged road which widens into a car park.

Access by Bus: On the N°7 **Yé** bus, from **Maguez**, ask for **Las Rositas** and the driver will drop you at the start of the lane. If you miss this stop, then alight in **Yé** by the unusual bar - the walk back to the **Las Rositas** junction is no hardship.

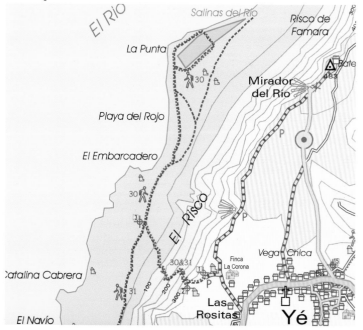

From the car park (Wp.1 0M) we walk along the path past pleasant rocky scenery before starting to drop down a staired descent, views opening up over the straights to **Isla Graciosa**. The stairs bring us to a stone built *mirador* by an electricity pylon (Wp.2). Along with the beautiful views this is also your decision point. Far below us are the multi-hued *salinas* salt pans, while the path drops straight down the cliffs; an intensely steep descent requiring careful footwork on the zigzagging trail, and an equally intense 'puff & grunt' ascent on your return.

Contemplating the descent

From the *mirador*, our whole route is laid out below us, and it is decision time. This is easily the steepest descent and ascent on the island, requiring concentration all the way down. Concentrating on where you are putting your feet helps combat any sense of vertigo, as does facing the cliff when taking breaks. However if it is windy, or any sign of bad weather, we would suggest you save this route for another day.

On the zigzag descent

We set off, stepping down through the small, steep zigzags in a near vertical descent. This continues down for over a hundred metres before there is any relaxation on a moderate slope, and then we tackle a second series of small, steep zigzags for another hundred metres of near-vertical descent. Finally, our trail comes to a steady descent, and a fainter trail goes left offering a short cut on our **Risco de Famara** route. Keeping straight on we are on easy walking to come down to a T-junction with a track (Wp.3 48M).

Having made the descent, we are now free to explore the beach and salt pans, either by keeping to the track (N) or using the tracery of small paths that have been walked. The track ends at an electricity transformer that sends power over to **La Graciosa** via a sea bed cable. **Salinas del Río** is no longer in production, but at least its 'pans' are still here, and the evaporating sea water creates some beautiful colours. Cozzie-optional swimming is popular at the beach of **Playa del Risco**, so do indulge yourself if you wish. This is a beautiful isolated region, where we usually see only eco-responsible walkers, so it's an unwelcome surprise to find so much litter, in particular broken bottles, detracting from its natural beauty.

At some stage we have to remember that civilisation in the form of our car is at the top of that cliff. Personally we prefer the ascent to the knee-jarring descent, despite its 'puff & grunt' nature requiring a lot of recovery stops, but like it or hate it, it has got to be climbed. At least, when we get back to the *mirador* we certainly have a well-earned sense of achievement.

31. EL RISCO DE FAMARA

Lanzarote's classic walking route is not for the faint hearted, as it starts with that awesome descent used for our **Salinas del Río** route. The central part of the route is on an amazing path that has been hacked and dynamited out of the sheer cliff face of the **Famara** - quite why anyone should have undertaken such a labour is a mystery, but it has given us a route that is spectacular in any walker's lexicon. You can see a glimpse of this path from the **Mirador de Haría** on Walk 25; medium danger of vertigo on the descent and on the cliff face path.

Best walked in the early morning, when most of the route is in shade from the cliffs.

If this route has a problem, it's because it is long and linear between two places not best served by public transport. Best approach is to use two cars between four to eight walkers. Park one car at **La Caleta** or **Famara** with half the party, and drive the other car to **Yé** and park at the end of the stone-flagged road as for Walk 30. When you meet up, remember to exchange car keys (see P.16 for a full explanation)

Access by Car: Park at the end of the stone flagged road outside **Yé** (see Walk 30). When you reach **La Caleta** ask in the bars if they will call you a taxi for the trip back to **Yé**.

Access by Bus: a bit laborious, but can be done on bus N°7 from **Arrecife** or **Teguise** to **Yé**, or on N°20 to **Caleta de Famara**. Again, you are likely to need a taxi at the end of your route as there are few buses in these locations.

> **Short Walk**
> While not really a short walk, we suggest that you walk to **Punta del Roque** (Wp.5) and return. This is still four hours, but you do arrive back at your car.

Assuming we are in the downward group, we start off from the parking area (Wp.1 0M) outside **Yé** to walk down to the *mirador* (Wp.2) and tackle the descent down to the T-junction with the track (Wp.3 48M). Here we turn left (S) to start the steady ascent up the old track, which climbs for a hundred metres to come back under the main cliffs (Wp.4 90M) and the cliff face section.

This path is remarkable, having been cut into the hardest rock on Lanzarote. We continue gradually uphill taking great care on any scree-covered sections, and

The descent down to the T-junction

El Risco de Famara

whenever our route crosses gullies in the cliff face. It is steadily onwards and upwards until we cross a series of gullies to reach the trail's summit at **Punta del Roque** (Wp.5 126M) to be met by the spectacular view over **Famara** and **La Caleta**.

From **Punta del Roque** our trail slowly descends, but you are hardly likely to notice the gradient as we marvel at the path's construction, almost tunnelled along the cliff face in places, plus the views which are just spectacular. After what seems like a lifetime suspended alongside the **Risco de Famara**, our trail returns to normality (Wp.6 217M) as it becomes a scree-covered picky descent down towards a water tank and a house.

Down past the water tank, we come to the house (Wp.7 233M) set at the entrance of a tunnel that used to connect the pumping station to **Haría**. Until quite recently you could walk through the tunnel to **Haría**, but now it is closed off and locked.

From the 'tunnel' house we have a choice of routes to **La Caleta**. We

On the beach at 244 minutes

Mirador del
Risco
de Famara

Los Mariscales

Montañ
Ganado
588

Haria
Teguise

31

10

31&3

584•

8

Galería
de Famara

32

Military
Radomes

600

Peñas del
Chache 675

11

7

de

Famara

600

ya de Famara

32

6

El Risco de Famara

400

300

5

3

32

200

1

amara

4

26

2

could stay on the track running below the cliffs, our upward route on Walk 32, or take the track which runs down to the sea front pumping house which takes us to the abandoned structure (Wp.8 244M).

On Walk 32 we kept to the track which runs just inland of the beach, so this time we divert onto the beach for a sea-spray stroll along the very sea front to pass **Famara**'s unusual housing and arrive gratefully in **La Caleta** (Wp.9 320M).

31. FAMARA CIRCULAR

El Risco de Famara provides a dramatic backdrop to this easy route along the base of the cliffs before descending to beach level and returning on an easy track. Easy that is, if the wind is not blowing. **Famara** is famous for its wind and when it blows, this easy beach-side walk is transformed into a struggle through a desert sandstorm.

If you walk this route in the morning, then the first half will be shaded by the tall cliffs. The earlier you start, the shadier the route is - much more refreshing than walking in the blazing intensity of the afternoon.

Access by Car: Park on the roadside just before reaching the **Famara** bungalow development.

Access by Bus: Route Nº20 offers a limited service to **Caleta de Famara**.

From the corner of the **Famara** development (Wp.1 0M) we head up the private road (SE) on an easy stroll past the walled squat bungalows. Ahead and above are the golf ball radomes on a ridge behind the main **Famara** cliffs as we come up to a sign for the reception (Wp.2). From here you could continue ahead, signed '*playa*', to skirt the development, but our choice is to go left (NE) to walk between the square bungalows with curved walls. Past the reception, bar and shop, we reach the far side of the development (Wp.3 12M) where we go right (SE) to walk uphill, going right and left at top of **Calle Aguamala** to come up between the houses and meet the beach road just beyond a barrier (Wp.4 17M). Interesting to note the subtle change in architectural style between the lower and higher bungalows; below reception are square houses with curved walls, while above reception, the houses are curved with straight walls.

Going left on the broad dirt track (NE), we are back to easy strolling as we come down past little gobbets of lava rock beside the route; insignificant beside the impressive cliffs, but nevertheless large rocks in their own right. When the main track swings towards the beach (Wp.5 25M) - our short stroll option - we continue straight ahead on a steady ascent that brings us up to pass an old farmstead in the course of restoration (Wp.6 27M), and on our right a cobbled trail leads up to a second house and its veritable oasis of a walled garden amongst this barren wilderness.

Along the track, we pass a walled threshing circle before coming below an old ruin (Wp.7), the track getting rougher as we ascend. It is steadily uphill towards an intriguing white building that peeks out from behind the ridges which run down from the towering cliffs. As we move along below the cliffs, the surroundings become more floriferous, the slopes becoming covered in tabaiba and other endemic plants; even the giant dandelion-like sonchus thrives here, showing that this is a 'wet' area compared to the barren land earlier in the route.

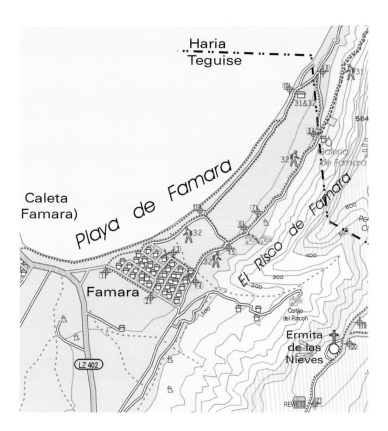

Round a small headland, the house comes back into view, a large spoil heap giving a clue as to what lies ahead. We come up beside the little house (Wp.8 47M 136 metres) to find that it sits at the entrance to a tunnel into the cliffs.

In this unusual elevated position, we can appreciate both the towering cliffs and the beach curving around to **La Caleta**. A track leads up behind the house past an old white water tank (NNE), the cliff face route to **Yé**. Down below us beside the beach track stands a white building which is our next destination.

Wonderful views from the spoil heap

We take the downhill track behind the house (N), more a path than a dirt road with a rubble-ised surface requiring careful footwork. As we pick our way down, the aquamarine sea crashes onto rock 'pimples', and the beach raises its own sea mist. Our track becomes increasingly rubble strewn as we come to a steep path down to our left, a possible short cut to miss a loop of the track, while we stay on the track to drop down to a junction (Wp.9 60M). Going left (SW) we continue dropping down towards the white building on the rubble-

... the aquamarine sea crashes onto rock 'pimples' ...

strewn track. Passing the lower end of the short cut path), we pick our way down to a junction (Wp.10) with the *playa* track. At last we are back to comfortable strolling, to come along to the old pumping house and a beach-side pillbox (Wp.11 68M).

The final section needs hardly any description. You could walk along the pebble beach, but our choice is to take the *playa* track for an easy stroll (SE). Easy that is, if it isn't windy, when it can be more like fighting our way through a desert storm than an easy stroll. When the *playa* track swings inland (Wp.12), keep straight ahead on a minor track (SE) which almost peters out before reaching the corner of the bungalows. Here, you could cut through the houses or keep to the sand dunes and beach before curving round the beach side of **Famara** to come onto the road near your car (100M).

GPS Waypoints are quoted for the WGS84 datum used on the Lanzarote Tour & Trail Super-Durable Map, from which the map sections used in Walk! Lanzarote are taken. WGS84 is the default datum for GPS units by the main GPS manufacturers.

To input the waypoints into your gps set the 'location format' to 'hddd°.mm.mmm'. While we quote waypoints to four places of decimals, as recorded during our research, you might only be able to input to three places of decimals, depending on your GPS unit.

DWG are publishing PNFs (Personal Navigator Files) of the GPS tracks and waypoints from all of our walking research as a CD. These PNFs are in Oziexplorer .plt and .wpt format which can be used with Oziexplorer, GPSU and Gartrip software. In addition to Lanzarote the CD will also contain Tenerife, La Gomera, Madeira, Mallorca, Alpujarras, Sierra de Aracena GPS tracks and waypoints.

See our website:

www.walking.demon.co.uk

- for more information, and also the notes on using GPS on Lanzarote; see pages 22 and 23.

1. PUERTO DEL CARMEN - ARRECIFE			2. COASTAL DISCOVERY			3. COASTAL PROMENADE - COSTA TEGUISE		
Wp	N	W	Wp	N	W	Wp	N	W
1	28 55.7784	13 37.4574	1	28 55.2894	13 40.3536	1	28 59.2956	13 30.2214
2	28 55.9296	13 37.0476	2	28 55.3218	13 40.5822	2	28 59.4792	13 29.8614
3	28 55.9446	13 36.9666	3	28 55.2768	13 40.8042	3	28 59.5878	13 29.7540
4	28 56.0544	13 36.7986	4	28 55.2594	13 40.8594	4	28 59.6070	13 29.6916
5	28 56.0916	13 36.5916	5	28 55.2498	13 41.2410	5	28 59.6190	13 29.6046
6	28 56.4732	13 36.3972	6	28 55.2996	13 41.2140	6	28 59.5692	13 29.4198
7	28 56.6256	13 36.2256	7	28 55.0847	13 42.0175	7	28 59.5644	13 29.2356
8	28 56.9088	13 35.9034	8	28 55.2654	13 42.0588	8	28 59.6910	13 29.2206
9	28 56.9898	13 35.8086	9	28 55.1142	13 42.2082	9	28 59.8428	13 29.3466
10	28 56.9940	13 35.6706	10	28 54.9531	13 42.5937	10	29 00.0090	13 29.2134
11	28 57.0948	13 35.3616	11	28 54.9496	13 42.6682	11	28 59.9712	13 29.0178
12	28 57.0816	13 35.0952	12	28 54.9734	13 42.7114	12	28 59.9976	13 28.9224
13	28 57.1548	13 35.0064	13	28 54.4982	13 43.5339	13	29 00.1476	13 28.9014
14	28 57.2490	13 34.9746	14	28 54.4255	13 43.8788	14	29 00.2988	13 28.6896
15	28 57.2154	13 34.7106				15	29 00.4524	13 28.8138
16	28 57.2430	13 34.6032				16	29 00.0984	13 29.1720
17	28 57.3126	13 34.5120						
18	28 57.3222	13 34.4580						
19	28 57.2856	13 34.3308						
20	28 57.2808	13 34.2654						
21	28 57.2826	13 33.9300						
22	28 57.3696	13 33.7494						
23	28 57.3834	13 33.5700						
24	28 57.4746	13 33.6510						

4. SUNDAY MARKET SPECIAL - CAMINO EL CHARCO

Wp	N	W
1	29 03.5790	13 33.3996
2	29 03.2880	13 33.0660
3	29 03.0792	13 32.7906
4	29 03.1560	13 32.2680
5	29 03.3072	13 32.1474
6	29 03.2520	13 31.9608
7	29 03.2760	13 31.8714
8	19 03.3102	13 31.7568
9	29 03.2736	13 31.6764
10	29 03.2556	13 31.6614
11	29 03.1680	13 31.5354
12	29 02.9652	13 31.0548
13	29 02.7798	13 30.8622
14	29 02.6370	13 30.5766
15	29 02.7906	13 30.3978
16	29 02.6376	13 30.5586
17	29 02.5308	13 30.4698
18	29 02.2290	13 30.1542
19	29 02.1492	13 30.0234
20	29 01.9638	13 29.8140
21	29 01.6770	13 29.6016
22	29 00.8634	13 29.1954
23	29 00.7056	13 29.3358

5. MONTAÑA CORONA

Wp	N	W
1	29 00.7386	13 29.3538
2	29 00.7764	13 29.6724
3	29 00.8946	13 29.7312
4	29 00.9936	13 29.7774
5	29 01.0536	13 29.8152
6	29 01.1040	13 29.8482
7	29 01.1502	13 29.8932
8	29 01.2582	13 30.0450
9	29 01.3470	13 30.0498
10	29 01.4760	13 29.9676
11	29 01.4814	13 29.9172
12	29 01.4142	13 29.8194
13	29 01.3698	13 29.7360
14	29 01.4298	13 29.7426
15	29 01.4118	13 29.6568
16	29 01.3836	13 29.6226
17	29 01.2990	13 29.6022
18	29 01.2792	13 29.5938
19	29 01.2534	13 29.6010
20	29 01.2270	13 29.6208
21	29 01.0548	13 29.6622
22	29 01.0722	13 29.6124
23	29 00.9198	13 29.4996
24	29 00.8874	13 29.4456
25	29 00.8712	13 29.4030

6. COASTAL PROMENADE - PLAYA BLANCA WEST

Wp	N	W
1	28 51.5382	13 50.1492
2	28 51.3792	13 50.4150
3	28 51.4992	13 50.5920
4	28 51.7212	13 51.2130
5	28 51.7236	13 51.2910
6	28 51.6624	13 51.4254
7	28 51.6900	13 51.6156
8	28 51.5634	13 51.9204

7. COASTAL PROMENADE - PLAYA BLANCA EAST

Wp	N	W
1	28 51.5574	13 48.1494
2	28 51.5502	13 48.1662
3	28 51.4584	13 48.3900
4	28 51.4416	13 48.5586
5	28 51.4104	13 48.6348
6	28 51.4086	13 48.7290
7	28 51.5694	13 48.9504
8	28 51.6918	13 49.1454
9	28 51.7134	13 49.2762
10	28 51.6606	13 50.0670

8. MONTAÑA ROJA

Wp	N	W
1	28 52.1772	13 50.9028
2	28 52.2126	13 50.9280
3	28 52.2390	13 51.0324
4	28 52.2348	13 51.2202
5	28 52.1544	13 51.2094
6	28 52.1298	13 51.2226
7	28 52.0962	13 51.3006
8	28 52.0950	13 51.4020
9	28 52.1196	13 51.4656
10	28 52.1532	13 51.4908
11	28 52.2624	13 51.2484

9 PAPAGAYO BEACH

Wp	N	W
1	28 51.6354	13 47.8392
2	28 51.5640	13 47.8296
3	28 51.4374	13 47.6958
4	28 51.3756	13 47.6772
5	28 51.2886	13 47.6082
6	28 51.1992	13 47.5188
7	28 50.9922	13 47.4180
8	28 50.9418	13 47.4126
9	28 50.8032	13 47.3406
10	28 50.6862	13 47.2710
11	28 50.5992	13 47.2974
12	28 50.9148	13 47.3148
13	28 51.3330	13 47.4870

10 PEÑA DEL RUBICÓN

Wp	N	W
1	28 51.5616	13 51.9180
2	28 51.3432	13 52.3422
3	28 51.3708	13 52.3992
4	28 51.4458	13 52.4586
5	28 51.6396	13 52.5480
6	28 51.9384	13 52.5462
7	28 52.3242	13 52.4760
8	28 52.7202	13 52.5750
9	28 52.8954	13 52.7370
10	28 53.0340	13 52.8030
11	28 53.5134	13 52.4148

11. YAIZA'S VOLCANIC GARDENS

Wp	N	W
1	28 57.1410	13 45.9192
2	28 57.0414	13 45.9360
3	28 57.0438	13 46.0560
4	28 56.9694	13 46.2180
5	28 57.0780	13 46.2762
6	28 57.2034	13 46.3368
7	28 57.0762	13 46.6104
8	28 57.2508	13 46.3632

12. ATALAYA DE FEMÉS LINEAR

Wp	N	W
1	28 57.1338	13 45.9162
2	28 57.0246	13 45.9030
3	28 56.9070	13 45.7248
4	28 56.4696	13 45.4554
5	28 56.1540	13 45.5940
6	28 56.0400	13 45.7068
7	28 55.2858	13 46.8558
8	28 55.1304	13 47.0358
9	28 55.0458	13 46.7460
10	28 55.0032	13 46.5828
11	28 54.9672	13 46.5816
12	28 54.7962	13 46.7544
13	28 54.8748	13 46.6032
14	28 55.2738	13 46.1304
15	28 54.4652	13 45.9888
16	28 55.7400	13 45.8166
17	28 55.7856	13 45.7710
18	28 55.8360	13 45.7344
19	28 55.8576	13 45.7230
20	28 55.8648	13 45.7158
21	28 55.8696	13 45.6636
22	28 55.9482	13 45.7308

13. ATALAYA DE FEMÉS CIRCUIT

Wp	N	W
1	28 54.7962	13 46.7544
2	28 54.8748	13 46.6032
3	28 55.0956	13 46.3764
4	28 55.2738	13 46.1304
5	28 55.4652	13 45.9888
6	28 55.7400	13 45.8166
7	28 55.7856	13 45.7710
8	28 55.8360	13 45.7344
9	28 55.8576	13 45.7230
10	28 55.8648	13 45.7158
11	28 55.8696	13 45.6636
12	28 55.9482	13 45.7308
13	28 55.2858	13 46.8558
14	28 55.1304	13 47.0358
15	28 55.0458	13 46.7460
16	28 55.0032	13 46.5828
17	28 54.9672	13 46.5816

14. THE HIDDEN BARRANCOS

Wp	N	W
1	28 54.7722	13 46.7508
2	28 54.6690	13 46.7274
3	28 54.6570	13 46.6950
4	28 54.6264	13 46.6518
5	28 54.4326	13 46.6428
6	28 54.3720	13 46.3938
7	28 54.3282	13 46.3002
8	28 54.2628	13 46.1892
9	28 54.1752	13 45.9768
10	28 54.1308	13 45.9804
11	28 54.1170	13 45.7722
12	28 54.0942	13 45.7020
13	28 54.0588	13 45.6354
14	28 53.9238	13 46.0734
15	28 53.9442	13 46.0752
16	28 53.8680	13 46.3026
17	28 53.7822	13 46.2828
18	28 53.7258	13 46.2732
19	28 53.8014	13 46.4400
20	28 53.9118	13 46.7382
21	28 53.9874	13 46.8018
22	28 54.3096	13 46.8060
23	28 54.5154	13 46.7928

15. FEMÉS RIDGE

Wp	N	W
1	28 54.7818	13 46.7658
2	28 54.6738	13 46.7274
3	28 54.6576	13 46.6944
4	28 54.6492	13 46.6500
5	28 54.6414	13 46.4868
6	28 54.7020	13 46.3152
7	28 54.7272	13 46.2294
8	28 54.8688	13 46.0194
9	28 55.1484	13 45.7572
10	28 55.1742	13 45.6912
11	28 55.1322	13 45.7026
12	28 55.0278	13 45.5796
13	28 54.8970	13 45.4830
14	28 54.7608	13 45.3798
15	28 54.8112	13 45.5652
16	28 54.4398	13 45.6072
17	28 54.3858	13 45.9054
18	28 54.3750	13 46.1766
19	28 54.4128	13 46.4532
20	28 54.4098	13 46.5582
21	28 54.4326	13 46.6410

16. FEMÉS TO PLAYA BLANCA

Wp	N	W
1	28 54.7974	13 46.7460
2	28 54.6738	13 46.7202
3	28 54.6486	13 46.6524
4	28 54.6210	13 46.7010
5	28 54.3168	13 46.8060
6	28 53.9838	13 46.8054
7	28 53.9280	13 46.9218
8	28 53.3592	13 46.2918
9	28 53.0748	13 45.7950
10	28 52.7880	13 45.2412
11	28 52.3602	13 45.7458
12	28 51.7578	13 46.2258
13	28 51.6612	13 46.2954
14	28 50.6544	13 47.2590

17. FEMÉS TO PLAYA QUEMADA

Wp	N	W
1	28 54.7962	13 46.7418
2	28 54.6768	13 46.7256
3	28 54.6522	13 46.6548
4	28 54.6306	13 46.6548
5	28 54.4314	13 46.6476
6	28 54.4086	13 46.4496
7	28 54.3846	13 45.9048
8	28 54.4344	13 45.6294
9	28 54.2772	13 45.2256
10	28 54.1554	13 44.8500
11	28 54.0714	13 44.7486
12	28 54.0846	13 44.5596
13	28 54.3324	13 44.4234
14	28 54.3978	13 44.2416
15	28 54.4362	13 44.1924
16	28 54.4398	13 44.0442
17	28 54.4308	13 43.9836
18	28 54.4338	13 43.8804

18. TREMESANA GUIIDED WALK

Wp	N	W
1	28 59.1494	13 47.9747
2	28 58.0119	13 46.1206

19.
MONTAÑA CUERVO - A GEM
IN LANZAROTE'S CROWN

Wp	N	W
1	28 59.5674	13 41.1024
2	28 59.4894	13 41.3808
3	28 59.5830	13 41.4894
4	28 59.5230	13 41.5170
5	28 59.5182	13 41.5836
6	28 59.5800	13 41.6406
7	28 59.4960	13 41.7438
8	28 59.4480	13 41.8572
9	28 59.3520	13 41.7294
10	28 59.4414	13 41.4534
11	28 59.5050	13 41.3370

20.
A PATH BETWEEN TWO
SEAS - THE TIMANFAYA
COASTAL PATH

Wp	N	W
1	29 03.7390	13 46.4203
2	29 59.5442	13 49.0825
3	28 59.3694	13 49.0306
4	28 59.1605	13 48.8771

21.
LA GÉRIA

Wp	N	W
1	28 56.9490	13 44.6406
2	28 56.9010	13 44.4972
3	28 57.1602	13 44.2506
4	28 57.4074	13 42.9570
5	28 57.3552	13 42.7032
6	28 57.3702	13 42.5586
7	28 57.1590	13 42.7530
8	28 57.0138	13 43.0368
9	28 57.4482	13 42.3774
10	28 57.0852	13 41.9934
11	28 56.9886	13 41.9568
12	28 56.9190	13 41.8002
13	28 56.6178	13 41.6484
14	28 56.4030	13 41.6262
15	28 56.2356	13 41.4546
16	28 56.1666	13 41.1354
17	28 55.5420	13 41.2680
18	28 55.3026	13 41.2182

22.
PLAYA DEL POZO

Wp	N	W
1	28 54.4590	13 44.1822
2	28 54.3984	13 44.2452
3	28 54.3720	13 44.3106
4	28 54.3366	13 44.3874
5	28 54.3306	13 44.3874
6	28 54.3216	13 44.4156
7	28 54.2670	13 44.4552
8	28 54.2568	13 44.4750
9	28 54.1518	13 44.4894
10	28 54.0822	13 44.5464
11	28 54.0618	13 44.6184
12	28 54.0426	13 44.6448
13	28 53.9904	13 44.6244
14	28 53.8986	13 44.6874
15	28 54.4458	13 44.4360
16	28 54.4644	13 44.3406

24.
THE FORGOTTEN TRAIL

Wp	N	W
1	29 08.7678	13 29.9988
2	29 08.7456	13 30.0744
3	29 08.6010	13 30.1500
4	29 08.4858	13 30.2130
5	29 08.4294	13 30.2448
6	29 08.4096	13 30.2562
7	29 08.2836	13 30.3738
8	29 08.0988	13 30.6180
9	29 07.9668	13 30.8070
10	29 07.9062	13 30.9534
11	29 07.8930	13 30.9390
12	29 07.8852	13 30.9684
13	29 07.8690	13 30.9342
14	29 07.7880	13 30.9240
15	29 07.7775	13 30.9324
16	29 07.7598	13 30.9282

25.
CIRCUIT OF HARÍA

Wp	N	W
1	29 08.7936	13 29.9598
2	29 09.0114	13 30.0264
3	29 09.0516	13 30.0888
4	29 09.0210	13 30.4848
5	29 09.0270	13 30.5490
6	29 09.0138	13 30.7182
7	29 09.0264	13 30.8598
8	29 08.9466	13 30.9246
9	29 08.9508	13 30.9666
10	29 08.9460	13 30.9792
11	29 08.9358	13 31.0074
12	29 08.9070	13 31.1544
13	29 08.7138	13 31.1562
14	29 08.4042	13 30.7092
15	29 08.1906	13 30.9204
16	29 08.1504	13 30.7242
17	29 08.1948	13 30.6504
18	29 08.4402	13 30.3720

26.
CAPITAL ROUTE - HARÍA
TO TEGUISE

Wp	N	W
1	29 08.7678	13 29.9988
2	29 08.7456	13 30.0744
3	29 08.6010	13 30.1500
4	29 08.4858	13 30.2130
5	29 08.4294	13 30.2448
6	29 08.4096	13 30.2562
7	29 08.2836	13 30.3738
8	29 08.0988	13 30.6180
9	29 07.9668	13 30.8070
10	29 07.9062	13 30.9534
11	29 07.8930	13 30.9390
12	29 07.8852	13 30.9684
13	29 07.8690	13 30.9342
14	29 07.7880	13 30.9240
15	29 07.7741	13 30.9324
16	29 07.4886	13 30.9396
17	29 07.4394	13 30.9552
18	29 07.0350	13 31.1352
19	29 06.6072	13 31.5444
20	29 06.3840	13 31.6944
21	29 06.1320	13 31.8360
22	29 05.6268	13 32.1180
23	29 05.5470	13 32.2386
24	29 05.5860	13 32.3610
25	29 04.0938	13 32.5686
26	29 04.0164	13 32.7570
27	29 03.9072	13 33.1830
28	29 03.8346	13 33.2928
29	29 03.6012	13 33.5844

27. MALA TO TEGUISE

Wp	N	W
1	29 05.9916	13 28.1850
2	29 06.0528	13 28.4394
3	29 06.1104	13 28.6014
4	29 06.4836	13 28.8054
5	29 06.7968	13 29.5212
6	29 06.8898	13 29.6172
7	29 07.0068	13 29.7510
8	29 06.9798	13 29.9910
9	29 06.9108	13 30.2424
10	29 06.7188	13 30.2616
11	29 06.6402	13 30.2760
12	29 06.8028	13 30.8574
13	29 06.3990	13 30.8346
14	29 06.5034	13 31.6002
15	29 06.3840	13 31.6944
16	29 06.1266	13 31.8384
17	29 05.6364	13 32.0998
18	29 05.5471	13 32.2412
19	29 05.5881	13 32.3472
20	29 04.0901	13 32.5734
21	29 04.0271	13 32.7363
22	29 03.9169	13 33.1760
23	29 03.8277	13 33.2938

28. HELECHOS CIRCULAR

Wp	N	W
1	29 09.5460	13 29.7720
2	29 09.5520	13 29.6370
3	29 09.9276	13 29.5998
4	29 10.4832	13 29.2278
5	29 10.6932	13 29.4306
6	29 10.7082	13 29.4882
7	29 10.5864	13 29.8536
8	29 10.6566	13 29.9034
9	29 10.2198	13 30.5382
10	29 10.1388	13 30.7698
11	29 09.9600	13 30.7512
12	29 09.6582	13 30.9720
13	29 09.8976	13 30.6258
14	29 10.0686	13 30.5022
15	29 10.2090	13 30.2346
16	29 09.8328	13 30.3432
17	29 10.1106	13 30.2772
18	29 09.8340	13 30.0474
19	29 10.0068	13 29.8308
20	29 09.8790	13 29.8308
21	29 09.7536	13 29.7354

29. MÁGUEZ TO YÉ

Wp	N	W
1	29 09.5460	13 29.7720
2	29 09.5520	13 29.6370
3	29 09.9276	13 29.5998
4	29 10.4832	13 29.2278
5	29 10.5972	13 28.9944
6	29 11.0976	13 28.4106
7	29 11.3196	13 28.2594
8	29 11.6424	13 27.6408
9	29 11.8230	13 27.5166
10	29 12.0852	13 28.0080
11	29 12.1368	13 28.1652
12	29 12.1578	13 28.3086
13	29 12.0780	13 28.3908
14	29 12.0456	13 28.4088
15	29 11.8122	13 28.7070

30. SALINAS DEL RÍO

Wp	N	W
1	29 11.7906	13 29.5470
2	29 11.7414	13 29.6994
3	29 12.0804	13 29.9976

31. RISCO DE FAMARA

Wp	N	W
1	29 11.7906	13 29.5470
2	29 11.7414	13 29.6994
3	29 12.0804	13 29.9976
4	29 10.9554	13 30.3438
5	29 10.4394	13 30.8418
6	29 08.2074	13 31.4580
7	29 07.6584	13 31.7838
8	29 07.9290	13 31.9416
9	29 07.0080	13 33.8346

32. FAMARA CIRCULAR

Wp	N	W
1	29 06.9132	13 33.2004
2	29 06.7764	13 32.9256
3	29 06.9558	13 32.7828
4	29 06.8388	13 32.6418
5	29 07.0236	13 32.4132
6	29 07.0878	13 32.2944
7	29 07.1922	13 32.1792
8	29 07.6482	13 31.7868
9	29 08.0502	13 31.7706
10	29 07.9458	13 31.9014
11	29 07.9110	13 31.9494
12	29 07.2078	13 32.5614

MAPS

Lanzarote is awash with cheap tourist maps of dubious accuracy, none of which are of any help to the walker. The route maps used in this book are taken from our new **Lanzarote Tour & Trail Super-Durable Map** (Discovery Walking Guides Ltd. ISBN 1-899554-95-5 2004 £7.99/€11.99) which covers the whole island at 1:40,000 scale; naturally, we recommend our own map as the best, but when you see one we believe you will agree that this is a remarkable map.

IGN 1:25,000 and 1:50,000 scale official Ministerio de Fomento maps are available from **Libreria Villalobos** in **Arrecife** at the reasonable price of €3.20 each. Surprisingly, the 1:25,000 scale maps have very little information on them of use to walkers, as they do not show tracks or footpaths. And as a complete island set of these maps would cost you €32.00, you will be better of with our Lanzarote Tour & Trail Super-Durable Map at €11.99; it has more detail and it is Super-Durable, lasting many times longer than flimsy paper maps.

WALKING BOOKS & INFORMATION

It's funny how many walking guide books deliberately ignore all the other walking guide books. as though there was no other walking information available. Well, not us. We seek out everything there is to find concerning walking for our destinations. Admittedly, on Lanzarote this is not a lot, but here is our opinion on what books are available - and please remember this is *our* opinion on these publications.

Ruta de Caballos (Ayuntamiento de Yaiza Dept. of Educación y Cultura. Free)

These six photocopied sheets first introduced us to the region between **Playa Quemada** and **Femés** for our 'Hidden Barrancos' route back in '95. All these routes are now incorporated into **Walk! Lanzarote**, but do call in for a copy, so that the department realises just how important walking is to Lanzarote tourism; they are trying to attract riders for the local stables industry, hence the *caballos* (for horse riders) and not *senderismos* (walking routes). Collect.

Guía Oficial de Senderos de Lanzarote (Cabildo de Lanzarote (Island Government) 2002 €15)

160 pages (in Spanish) plus a box of route maps is a commendable effort by the island government to promote walking. Maps are good on technicality giving height profiles, distances, walking surface, gradients. However, we would argue with their 'difficulty' grading when they rate the easy track down

to **Papagayo** as 'medium' but the far trickier path around **Pico Redondo** as 'easy'.

Researched and written by three lads exploring the island, the book has a good feel, but is let down by not having a contents page or index. There are only 16 main routes, and that includes **Yaiza** and **San Bartolomé** town walks, but our main comment is on the choice of routes. No thought has been given to accessibility. Most routes involve a long linear hike, often well away from bus routes. Their only real circular route is **Yaiza** - **El Golfo** - **Yaiza** - all along tarmac roads! Some routes seem to have little point to them, except to cover the ground.

Having been quite damning so far (and one book shop told us they refused to stock the book because the routes were so bad!) we would nevertheless recommend this book if you speak a little Spanish. Bits and pieces of routes can be used, and the book has good background information on the island. Buy.

Landscapes of Lanzarote (Sunflower Books. 2000 £9.99, but see below)

128 pages plus pull-out map. One of the infamous 'blue book' series, supposedly by the equally infamous (in the Canary Islands anyway) Noel Rochford. Noel originally researched the Landscapes Canary Islands titles in the mid/late 80s, and those early editions were renowned for walking times so fast, you thought he had used a motorcycle. For the 2000 editions John Underwood has produced his own mapping, much clearer than the old edition. Updates are carried out by local walkers, Noel now being long gone from the islands, and the whole book style modernised

Generally, you won't go far wrong with this book. If we have a criticism, it is that the five separate coastal walks included as '16 Coastal walks' deserve more description, and that when a book appears in a brand new cover we would expect a lot of new content inside that cover. Hopefully, the next edition will benefit from having GPS Waypoints to go with the routes.

Walking in the Canary Islands: 2 East (Cicerone Press £12.00 2002)

235 pages, but only 55 of these relate to Lanzarote. Paddy Dillon is an experienced walking writer and Cicerone Press publish a massive pile of walking guide books; so why do we not like this one, and its companion **Walking in the Canary Islands 1: West** title.

Firstly, why carry 180 redundant pages around with you? Secondly, the mapping (in both books) is not worthy of the name and does not deserve to be called 'mapping'. If you had to navigate from these sketches, you would soon be in trouble.

With such truly awful maps, you would expect the detailed walk descriptions to make up for the lack of mapping, but they don't. Descriptions are fairly minimalist. There is not even one route timing included in any walk description, no compass directions at trail junctions, and certainly no GPS navigation. Routes seem to have been chosen on the basis of going on a big hike, typically in the range of 17 to 29 kilometres in length; one exception to this is the three page section given to the 3 kilometre **Timanfaya** guided walk.

No thought has been given to accessibility; we presume Paddy was dropped at his start point and picked up again at his finish point, but for us mortals getting back to our hire car is very important, and we would have liked to hear how he got back again, and not just leave us 29 kilometres from our start point! Paddy's route, **La Hoya** to **Yaiza** via **El Golfo** is 17 kilometres of tarmac roads - not what we would call a 'walking route'.

Rather like some of the routes, 'pointless' is our conclusion for a book that purports to cover three islands in detail but fails on all of them.

REFERENCE BOOKS

Plant Life
Plants & Flowers of Lanzarote (Discovery Walking Guides Ltd. ISBN 1-899554-18-1 £1.99) is a budget priced basic introduction to Lanzarote's plant life, both wild and cultivated.

Flores Silvestres de las Islas Canarias
This is the serious plantsperson must-have publication. David and Zoë Bramwell's impressive and comprehensive tome, published in Spanish by Editorial Rueda, is usually available in **Libreria Villalobos** in **Arrecife**. There is an English translation which was published in 2001 (ISBN 8472071294 £35), but not always available on the island.

Volcanoes
Los Volcanes de las Islas Canarias (II) Lanzarote y Fuerteventura
There is nothing in English which goes into much detail about Lanzarote's volcanoes, but the enthusiast might look for this publication by Araña, Vicente and Carracedo, published by Editorial Rueda. Ask in **Libreria Villalobos** in **Arrecife**.

César Manrique
Fundación de César Manrique
If you want to know more about the man and his legacy, you need this publication(author Simon Marchan Fiz, published by Opus £25). It's available in English translation and can be found on amazon.co.uk., or may be in the **Libreria Villalobos** in **Arrecife**.

Coastline Guide
Coastline Aeroguide Eastern Canary Islands
This is one of a fascinating series of books combining aerial photographs with background information on various island destinations. **Coastline Aeroguide**

Eastern Canary Islands covers Gran Canaria, Fuerteventura and Lanzarote. An English translation is Published by Geoplaneta (ISBN 8-40803165-1 1999 around £25) Not easy to get hold of, but look in the **Arrecife Airport** bookshop (airside newsagents) or try in **Libreria Villalobos** in **Arrecife**.

This glossary contains Spanish and Canarian words found in the text (shown in *italics*), plus other local words that you may encounter.

a

abandonado	abandoned
abierto	open
acantilado	cliff
agua	water
agua no potable	water (not drinkable)
agua potable	drinking water
aljibe	sunken water tank
alto	high
aparcamiento	parking
arepa/arepera	deep fried savoury snack/bar specialising in arepas
autopista	main road, motorway
ayuntamiento	town hall

b

bajo	low
barranco	ravine
bocadillo	bread roll
bodegón	inn
buceo	scuba diving

c

cabezo	peak, summit
cabra	goat
café	coffee
caldera	collapsed cone (volcanic area)
calima	suspended dust brought in by hot east winds
calle	street
camino	trail, path, track
camino particular	private road
camino real	old donkey trail (lit. royal road)
carne	meat
carretera	main road
casa	house
casa rural	country house accommodation to let
caserío	hamlet, village
castillo	castle
cementario	cemetery
centro comercial	shopping centre
cerrado	closed
cerveza (caña, jarra, presión, lata)	beer (small, large, draught, can)
charco	pool
choza	shelter
clinica	clinic, hospital
colmena	bee hive

comida	food
conquistador	conqueror
cordillera	mountain range
correos	post office
cortijo	farmstead
costa	coast
coto privado de caza	private hunting area
Cruz Roja	Red Cross (medical aid)
cuesta	slope
cueva	cave
cumbre	summit

d

degollado	pass
derecha	right (direction)
desayuno	breakfast
desprendimiento	landslide

e

ermita	chapel
Espacio Naturaleza Protegido	protected area of natural beauty
estación de autobus/ guagua	bus station
este	east

f

farmacia	chemist
faro	lighthouse
fiesta	holiday, celebration
finca	farm, country house

g

gasolinera	petrol station
gofio	flour made from roasted maize, wheat or barley
guagua	bus
Guardia Civil	police
guia	guide

h

hornito	lava bubble
hostal	hostel, accommodation
hoya	depression (geological)
huevos	eggs

i

iglesia	church
información	information

isla	island		*playa*	beach
izquierda	left (direction)		*plaza*	square
			policia	police
j			*postre*	dessert
jameo	volcanic tube		*potaje*	thick soup
jamón	ham		*pozo*	well
			prohibido	
l			*el paso*	no entry
librería	bookshop		*puente*	bridge
llano	plain		*puerto*	port, mountain pass
lluvioso	rainy			
lomo	broad-backed ridge		**q**	
			queso	cheese
m				
Majos/Mahos	Lazarote's original inhabitants		**r**	
			risco	cliff
malpais	'bad lands' wild, barren countryside		*roque*	rock
			ruta	route
malvasia	Malmsey grapes and wine			
			s	
mapa	map		*salida*	exit
mareta	raised water collection tank		*salinas*	salt pans
			sangría	wine with fruit punch served in a jug of ice
mariscos	shellfish			
mercado	market		*senda*	path, track
mirador	lookout/viewing point		*sendero*	foot path
mojo	spicy sauce based on olive oil, tomatoes and chillis		*sin salida*	no through road/route
			sirocco	hot, dust-laden wind from Africa
montaña	mountain		*sur*	south
museo	museum			
			t	
n			*tapas*	bar snacks
norte	north		*té*	tea
nublado	cloudy		*tienda*	shop
			tipico	traditional bar/eating place
o				
oeste	west		*tormentoso*	stormy
oficina de			*torre*	tower
turismo	tourist office		*tubería*	water pipe
p			**v**	
paella	rice dish, usually with seafood or meat		*valle*	valley
			vega	meadow
panadería	bakery		*ventoso*	windy
papas	wrinkled potatoes		*vino (blanco,*	
arrugadas	(small potatoes in their skins cooked in salt water)		*tinto, rosado)*	wine (white, red, rosé)
			volcán	volcano
parapente	hang-glider			
parque eólico	wind farm		**z**	
pastelería	cake shop		*zocos*	crescent shaped vine enclosures (as seen in La Geria)
peligro	danger			
pensión	guesthouse		*zona recreativa*	recreation area
pescado	fish		*zumo/zumería*	freshly pressed fruit juice/juice bar
pico	peak			
picon	black volcanic rock/sand			
pista	dirt road/track			
pista (forestal)	forest road/track			

The following notes represent a random selection of activities available. Please note that they have not been tested by the authors. For other information, call in the friendly **Puerto del Carmen Tourist Office**, alongside the main beach (Tel: 928 513351 puertodelcarmen@tias.org). There are other tourist offices on the island but whenever we have called (within their published opening hours) they've been closed.

BIKE RENTAL

Bike Rental, Avenida de las Playas, C.C. Maritimo 25, Alto **Puerto del Carmen** Tel: 629 990755
Renner Bikes, **Puerto del Carmen** Tel: 629 990755
Cyclomaía, **Arrecife** Tel: 928 817535
Bike Station C.C. Maretas, **Costa Teguise**

BOAT TRIPS, FISHING TRIPS, TAXI-BOATS & FERRIES

Princesa Yaiza taxi-boat between **Playa Blanca** and **Papagayo Beach**, leaves **Playa Blanca** 10.00, 11.30, 13.30, 15.30, leaves **Papagayo Beach** 12.00, 14.00, 16.00 (€12 adults, €6 children
SubCat submarine-catamaran trips, **Puerto del Carmen** old port of **Varadero**, Tel: 928 510065 & 629 731293
Catlanza boat trips from **Puerto Calero** to **Papagayo**. Tel: 928 513022 info@catlanza.com www.catlanza.com
Marea Errota schooner from **Playa Blanca** to **Papagayo Beach**, Tel: 928 517633 mareaerrota@retemail.es
Fred Olsen's Buganvilla ferry between Lanzarote and Fuerteventura, leaves from **Playa Blanca** 08.00, 10.00, 14.00, 16.00, 18.00 and returns from **Corralejo** 09.00, 11.00, 15.00, 17.00, 19.00 Tel: 928 517266
Princesa Ico (Motobarco) trips to Fuerteventura and Isla de Lobos from **Puerto del Carmen** old port of **Varadero**, Tel: 928 514322
Ana Segundo (Motobarco) fishing trips from **Puerto del Carmen** old port of **Varadero**, Tel: 928 514322
Submarine Safaris from **Puerto Calero** Tel: 928 512898 subsafari@jet.es www.submarinesafaris.com
Lanzarote Fishing Club, **Puerto del Carmen**, Tel: 689 167956

WINDSURFING

Lanzarote Surf Company, **Costa Teguise**, Tel: 928 591974
Centro de Windsurfing, **Club La Santa**, Tel: 928 599999

SURFING

Escuela de Surf Franito, **Arrecife**, Tel: 928 806726
Tropical Feelings Surf School, **Famara**, Tel: 928 528668

HORSE RIDING

Lanzarote a Caballo (horse riding) on the LZ2, km.17, Tel 928 830314
alturin@alturin.com www.alturin.com
Centro Hípico Rancho Texas, **Puerto del Carmen**, Tel: 928 173247

GOLF

Club de Golf **Costa Teguise**, Tel: 928 591656

KARTING

Gran Karting Club Lanzarote, **Tías**, Tel: 619 759946
Go Karting San Bartolomé, **San Bartolomé**, Tel: 928 520022

DIVING

Safari Diving **Puerto del Carmen**, Tel: 928 511992
Centro de Buceo 'Toninas' (diving centre), Hotel Playa Flamingo, **Playa Blanca**, Tel: 928 517300
Lanzarote Dive Service, Avenida de las Playas, **Puerto del Carmen**, Tel: 928 510802 lanzarote@lanzarotedive.com
Club Buceo Punta Fariones **Órzola**, Tel: 928 842558
La Santa Sport Diving , **La Santa** Tel: 928 599999

MUSEUMS

Museo del Vino 'El Grifo' (Wine Museum) **Masdache** near **San Bartolom**é (free admission), Tel 928 524012 bodegas@elgrifo.com www.elgrifo.com
Museo de Arte Contemporáneo (Contemporary Art) in the Castillo de San José, **Arrecife**, Tel: 928 812321
Museo Etnográfico 'Tanit' artefacts from the island's original inhabitants, the Majos, **San Bartolomé**, Tel:928 802549 lanzarote@museotanit.com www.museotanit.com
Museo Agrícola 'El Patio' (Farming) with fruit & veg plots, farm animals, wine & cheese production in **Tiagua**, Tel: 928 529134 info@museoelpatio.com www.museoelpatio.com

- Please note that bus times are subject to change, and you should ask for the latest version on arrival. The Biosphere Information Office which almost faces you as you emerge from the baggage hall on arrival at Arrecife airport usually has copies to give away. Failing this, ask in the Puerto del Carmen Information office (near the beach).
- **Bold text** indicates places on or near our walking routes.
- Try www.turismolanzarote.com for latest information.
- Don't rely on catching the last bus back from a long walking day. It is advisable to carry taxi phone numbers and a mobile phone, just in case. Most villages have a public phone, otherwise, try a bar.

Nº	Mon - Fri	Saturday	Sun/Fiestas
1*			
ARRECIFE - COSTA TEGUISE	06.40, 07.00, 07.40, 08.00 Then every 20 mins at 20 past, 20 to & on the hour until 22.40 Last bus 23.40	06.40, 07.40, 08.40 Then at 10 past & 20 to the hour Last bus 23.40	As Saturday
COSTA TEGUISE - ARRECIFE	07.00, 07.20, 08.00 Then every 20 mins at 20 past, 20 to & on the hour until 23.00 Last bus 24.10	07.00, 08.00, 09.00 Then every 30 mins at half past & on the hour. Last bus 24.10	As Saturday

*With the exception of some late evening buses, these services continue to Puerto del Carmen.
Route:**Playa del Reducto** - Bus Station - Los Alonsos - Los Mármoles - Las Caletas - Hotel Oasis - Playa Roca - **Playa Bastián** - Pueblo Marinero - Lanzarote Gardens - Hotel Salinas

2**			
ARRECIFE - PUERTO DEL CARMEN	From 06.20 to 23.20 (last bus) on the hour, at 20 past & at 20 to the hour. The following continue to **Puerto Calero**: 07.00, 09.00, 11.20, 15.00, 19.40 23.20	06.20, 07.20, 07.50 08.20, 09.20 Then at 20 past and 10 to every hour until 22.20 Last bus 23.20 The following continue to **Puerto Calero**: 07.20, 10.20, 11.50, 14.50 19.50, 23.20	As Saturday
PUERTO DEL CARMEN - ARRECIFE	From 07.00 to 22.20 on the hour & at 20 past & 20 to the hour. Last buses 23.00, 24.10. The following continue to **Pto Calero** 07.40, 09.40, 12.00, 15.40, 20.20	07.00, 08.00, then on the hour & half-hour until 23.30. Last bus 24.10	As Saturday

**With the exception of some late evening buses, these services continue to Costa Teguise.
Route: Los Alonsos - Bus Station - **Playa del Reducto** - Crossroads Playa Honda - **Matagorda** - Hotel Jameos - Costa Mar - Hotel San Antonio - Arena Dorada - Los Fariones - Costa Volcán - Balcón del Mar - **Puerto Calero**

4			
ARRECIFE - AIRPORT - PLAYA HONDA - ARRECIFE	From 07.10 to 22.40 (last bus), at 10 past & 20 to every hour.	From 08.40 to 22.40 (last bus) at 10 past & 20 to every hour.	As Saturday

	Mon - Fri	Saturday	Sun/Fiestas
AEROPUERTO - PLAYA HONDA - ARRECIFE	From 07.20 to 22.50 (last bus), at 20 past & 10 to every hour	From 08.50 to 22.50 (last bus) at 20 past & 10 to every hour	

Route: **Playa del Reducto** - Playa Honda crossroads - Airport - C/San Borondón, **Playa del Reducto**

Nº 5	Mon - Fri	Saturday	Sun/Fiestas
ARRECIFE - FEMÉS	08.00, 14.00, 17.45	No service	No service
FEMÉS - ARRECIFE	09.00, 18.30	No service	No service

Route: Bus station - **Playa del Reducto** - Tías - Los Lirios - Conil - La Asomada - Mácher Petrol Station - Puerto Calero crossroads - Las Casitas de Femés - **Femés**

6			
ARRECIFE - PLAYA BLANCA	06.00, 07.00, 08.10, 08.30, 10.00 11.30, 13.00, 14.00, 15.15, 16.45 19.30, 20.15	06.50, 09.10, 12.00 14.30, 16.50, 19.40	06.50, 08.00 09.10, 12.00 13.30, 14.30 16.50, 19.40
PLAYA BLANCA - ARRECIFE	07.00, 07.45, 09.15, 10.00, 11.45 12.45, 13.45, 15.30, 16.15, 18.15 20.30, 21.30	08.00, 10.20, 13.10 15.40, 18.30, 20.50	08.00, 09.10 10.20, 13.10 14.40, 15.40 18.30, 20.50

Departures shown in purple call at only limited places for a semi-express journey.
Route: Bus Station - **Playa del Reducto** - Crossroads Playa Honda - Tías - Puente Los Lirios - Football Ground - Costa Volcán - Balcón del Mar - Mácher - Crossroads Puerto Calero - Uga Church - **Yaiza** - La Hoya - **Playa Blanca - Port, Playa Blanca**

7			
ARRECIFE - MÁGUEZ	08.00, 10.00, 12.30, 14.30, 18.00 20.00	08.00, 12.00, 14.00 20.00	07.30, 13.30 20.00
MÁGUEZ - ARRECIFE	06.50, 09.00, 11.30, 13.30, 15.30 19.00	07.00, 09.00, 13.00 21.00	08.45, 14.30 21.00

Departures shown in purple call at Punta Mujeres. Departures shown in green call at Los Valles. Departures shown in red call at Yé.

Routes: Bus Station - El Jamonal - César Manrique crossroads - Tahiche - Nazaret - **Teguise** - Los Valles - **Haría** - Máguez (additional stops on the Punta Mujeres and Yé routes include Guatiza - Cactus Garden - **Mala** - Arrieta - Punta Mujeres - **Yé**

9			
ARRECIFE - ÓRZOLA	07.40, 10.30, 15.30	07.40, 15.30	As Saturday
ÓRZOLA - ARRECIFE	08.30, 11.30, 16.30	08.30, 16.30	As Saturday

Route: Bus Station - César Manrique Crossroads - Tahiche - Nazaret - **Teguise** - Guatiza - Cactus Garden - **Mala** - Arrieta - Punta Mujeres - Jameos crossroads - Órzola

10			
ARRECIFE - LOS VALLES	10.00, 14.00, 19.00	No service	No service
LOS VALLES - ARRECIFE	07.00, 11.50, 15.50, 19.45	No service	No service

Route: Bus Station - César Manrique crossroads - Tahiche - Nazaret - Teguise - El Mojón - Los Valles

	Mon-Fri	Saturday	Sun/Fiestas
11			
COSTA TEGUISE - TEGUISE M'KT	No service	No service	09.00, 09.30 10.00, 10.15
TEGUISE M'KT - COSTA TEGUISE	No service	No service	12.00, 12.30 13.00, 13.15

Route: Hotel Oasis - **Playa Roca** - **Playa Bastián** - Pueblo Marinero - Lanzarote Gardens - **Hotel Salinas** - **Teguise** market

	Mon-Fri	Saturday	Sun/Fiestas
12			
PUERTO DEL CARMEN - TEGUISE M'KET	No service	No service	09.00, 09.30 10.00, 10.15
TEGUISE M'KET - PUERTO DEL CARMEN	No service	No service	12.00, 12.30 13.00, 13.15

Route:**Matagorda** - Hotel Jameos - Costa Mar - Hotel San Antonio - La Peñita - Los Fariones - Costa Volcán - Balcón del Mar - **Teguise** market

	Mon-Fri	Saturday	Sun/Fiestas
13			
PLAYA BLANCA - TEGUISE M'KET	No service	No service	09.00
TEGUISE M'KT - PLAYA BLANCA	No service	No service	13.00

Route: As route 6, then to **Teguise** market

	Mon-Fri	Saturday	Sun/Fiestas
14			
ARRECIFE - MT BLANCA	07.00, 13.50, 18.30	No service	No service
MT BLANCA - ARRECIFE	07.35, 14.20, 19.15	No service	No service

Route: Bus Station - **Playa del Reducto** - Playa Honda crossroads - C/ San Borondón - Avda. Las Palmeras - El Islote - Masdache - Montaña Blanca - Güime

	Mon-Fri	Saturday	Sun/Fiestas
16			
ARRECIFE - TINAJO - LA SANTA	06.15, 08.00, 10.15, 12.00, 14.00 15.45, 18.00, 20.00	07.45, 09.15, 11.50 13.50, 18.00	07.45, 13.30 18.00
LA SANTA - TINAJO - ARRECIFE	07.00, 08.50, 11.00, 13.00, 15.00 16.30, 19.00	07.00, 08.30, 10.00 12.50, 18.45	07.00, 08.30 18.45

Route:Bus Station - Arrecife - San Bartolomé - Mozaga - Tiagua - Mancha Blanca - Tinajo - La Santa - Club La Santa

	Mon-Fri	Saturday	Sun/Fiestas
17			
ARRECIFE - SÓO	14.00, 19.00	No service	No service
SÓO - ARRECIFE	07.10, 17.00	No service	No service

Route: Bus Station - San Bartolomé - Mozaga - Tao - Tiagua - Sóo

	Mon-Fri	Saturday	Sun/Fiestas
19			
ARRECIFE-CONIL - LA ASOMADA	07.00, 08.00, 14.00, 17.45	No service	No service
LA ASOMADA - CONIL-ARRECIFE	07.25, 09.15, 18.45	No service	No service

Route: Bus Station - **Playa del Reducto** - Tías - Conil - La Asomada - Mácher - Puerto Calero crossroads

20

ARRECIFE - SÓO - CALETA FAMARA	07.45, 14.00, 20.00	No service	No service
CALETA FAMARA -SÓO - ARRECIFE	07.00, 08.40, 17.00, 20,45	No service	No service

Route: Bus Station - Tahiche - Nazaret - **Teguise** - **Caleta de Famara**

Lanzarote

Tour & Trail

1:40,000 Scale Map

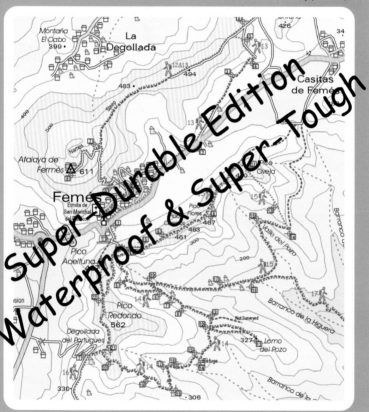

Super-Durable Edition
Waterproof & Super-Tough

Fully Detailed Walking Map
on Super-Durable polymer

£7.99 UK / €11.99 EU

Discovery Walking Guides Ltd
ISBN 1-899554-95-5
Copyright David & Ros Brawn

Tour & Trail Maps have been developed to meet the need for accurate, up to date, maps for regions covered by Discovery Walking Guides. At the core of each T&T map design is a comprehensive ground-level survey carried out on foot and by car. The survey results are then translated into our design programme, producing a digital vector-graphic database involving the organisation of several million pieces of information across a large number of 'layers' drawn digitally within our computers.

Once a digital vector-graphic database has been established, new developments such as new roads, tracks and buildings, can be quickly incorporated into the correct 'layer' of the database. Rapid updating, combined with state of the art 'file to plate' pre-press operation enables us to produce new editions of Tour & Trail Maps quickly and efficiently.

Tour & Trail Maps have Latitude/Longitude grids and datum information making them GPS compatible. DWG walking routes are clearly highlighted, along with their GPS Waypoints where space allows.

Since 2003, all new Tour & Trail Maps have been produced on a special high density polymer as Super-Durable editions which are waterproof and super tough, giving many seasons of use in the toughest conditions and outlasting paper maps many times over.

Tour & Trail Maps are available for:-
Lanzarote
La Gomera
Alpujarras
Madeira
Mallorca (North & Mountains)
Menorca
Gran Canaria Mountains

For Tenerife, we produce a **Tenerife Walkers' Maps** title available in both paper and Super-Durable editions.

Spending a lot of our time amongst dramatic landscapes, we appreciate the value of an accurately researched and well written walk description. Abroad in a foreign land is no place to find yourself lost and in danger. Knowing this, we operate a 'no compromise' policy to all of DWG's walking routes. We walk every route - repeatedly if necessary - to make sure that we have an accurate walk description. Then we try to write the detailed walk description in an inspirational tone so that you know how we felt on that route. We've slogged up that impossible looking ascent, marvelled at those panoramas, found paths through apparently pathless wilderness, have gratefully arrived at our destination. Its not always fun, but it has always been an adventure. Our GPS ground survey system means that we know exactly where we have been, and on Lanzarote you have good GPS reception on all routes except walk 23.

This 'no compromise' policy for our walking research has been much appreciated by users of DWG walking guides, as our post bag testifies. The result is that with a DWG guidebook you can confidently embark on the adventures it contains knowing that we have researched every route to the highest standard.

We still marvel at every 'Your guide made my holiday' letter we receive, just as we did at the first one we ever received. Bringing adventure and enjoyment to people is very pleasing, and we are very good listeners to what our readers would like to appear in a walk description. In Walk! Lanzarote you will find:-

- Walking route summary including Effort, Time, Distance, Ascents/Descents, and Refreshments
- Frequent timings so that you can judge your progress against the authors
- Fully detailed walk description
- Detailed colour maps for every walking route
- GPS Waypoints (grid references) for every key point on the route
- Full GPS Waypoint lists for walking routes
- Location Maps identifying all walks
- lots of useful background information

We haven't done all this just because Lanzarote is somewhere special, which it certainly is; this is our normal 'no compromise' approach to giving you everything you need in a walking guide book.

Now, go out there and enjoy it, safe in the knowledge that we have been there before. There are many easy routes for comfortable strolling. There are some energetic routes for serious walkers. Many routes can be linked together for those who crave 'all day' walking. With our descriptions, you will know which routes are for you, and all of them are an adventure.

David & Ros Brawn
Directors of Discovery Walking Guides Ltd
www.walking.demon.co.uk